Knowing the Cross

Knowing the Cross

Geoffrey Thomas

Reformation Heritage Books
Grand Rapids, Michigan

Knowing the Cross
© 2024 by Geoffrey Thomas

All rights reserved. No part of this book may be used or reproduced in any manner whatsoever without written permission except in the case of brief quotations embodied in critical articles and reviews. Direct your requests to the publisher at the following addresses:

Reformation Heritage Books
3070 29th St. SE, Grand Rapids, MI 49512
616-977-0889
orders@heritagebooks.org
www.heritagebooks.org

All Scripture quotations, unless otherwise indicated, are taken from the New King James Version®. Copyright © 1982 by Thomas Nelson. Used by permission. All rights reserved.

Scripture quotations marked KJV are taken from the King James Version. Public domain.

Scripture quotations marked NLT are taken from the Holy Bible, New Living Translation, copyright © 1996, 2004, 2007, 2013 by Tyndale House Foundation.

Printed in the United States of America
24 25 26 27 28 29/10 9 8 7 6 5 4 3 2 1

Library of Congress Cataloging-in-Publication Data

Names: Thomas, Geoff, 1938- author.
Title: Knowing the cross / Geoffrey Thomas.
Description: Grand Rapids, Michigan : Reformation Heritage Books, [2024] | Includes bibliographical references.
Identifiers: LCCN 2023054418 (print) | LCCN 2023054419 (ebook) | ISBN 9798886860900 (paperback) | ISBN 9798886860917 (epub)
Subjects: LCSH: Jesus Christ—Crucifixion.
Classification: LCC BT453 .T59 2024 (print) | LCC BT453 (ebook) | DDC 232.96/3—dc23/eng/20240125
LC record available at https://lccn.loc.gov/2023054418
LC ebook record available at https://lccn.loc.gov/2023054419

For additional Reformed literature, request a free book list from Reformation Heritage Books at the above regular or email address.

Dedicated to

Tommy and Linda Peaster
of Flora, Mississippi,
dear friends for forty years

CONTENTS

Introduction ix

1. Revelation 1
2. Imputation 9
3. Humiliation................................... 18
4. Retribution 25
5. Substitution................................... 33
6. Propitiation................................... 41
7. Redemption 47
8. Reconciliation................................. 54
9. Satisfaction 61
10. Destruction................................... 79
11. Foundation 101
12. Proclamation 116

Conclusion 123

INTRODUCTION

How little knowledge there is of the greatest event in world history. Even in the professing church there is much sheer sentimentalism, confusion, and ignorance as to what was happening when the Lord Jesus Christ, the Son of God, was nailed to a cross outside the walls of Jerusalem about two thousand years ago. For example, a friend of mine wrote to me about his concern for his mother:

> My widowed mother is now ninety and still lives in the same house which she has occupied for years. She is the granddaughter of Presbyterian missionaries in India, and the daughter of a Presbyterian pastor. She was a teacher of Religious Education in a grammar school for forty years. She had a stroke five years ago and now suffers with deteriorating eyesight, and yet she keeps busy. I bought her a Kindle and put the Bible alone on it because she had told me that what she wanted to read was the Old Testament. The Kindle permits the text to become considerably enlarged so that she is now able to read the Scriptures. We have had some interesting conversations. Last week for example we had a good chat, though it was all from her, with me listening. She finally

said, "Really I can't understand why God allowed his Son to go through all that and let him die."

Ninety years of church attendance, exemplary moral living, and even explaining the Scriptures to schoolchildren have passed, and yet she is still ignorant about the very heart of the claims of revealed religion concerning the death of the Lord Jesus Christ. The fact is that His crucifixion displays, more than any other event in history, the extraordinary character of the one true and living God, our Creator and our Sustainer, in whom we live and move and have our being, the Judge of the whole earth. The essence of the Christian faith is found in Jesus Christ and Him crucified.

Many in the professing church and in its pulpits are like this lady. How different is that grievous reality from the magnificent conviction of the first disciples of Jesus Christ, those witnesses of His life, crucifixion, and resurrection. The apostles thoroughly and accurately documented the Last Supper, the garden of Gethsemane, and the arrest, trials, whipping, crucifixion, burial, and appearances of the risen Lord Jesus. The apostle Paul stated that "the message of the cross is foolishness to those who are perishing, but to us who are being saved it is the power of God" (1 Cor. 1:18). These were dynamic men filled with a divine energy. "The people who know their God shall be strong, and carry out great exploits" (Dan. 11:32). It is the message of the cross that creates this strength of character and life. That message bifurcates the response of all who hear it: it is either total folly, like belief in the Loch Ness Monster, or it is the most relevant and life-transforming reality possible for men and women living on this planet.

The great heart of biblical Christianity, as preached by the apostle Paul—a word given to him by the Lord Jesus, inspired by the Holy Spirit, and mightily blessed by God—was this word of the death of the Lord Jesus Christ. There have been many great men in the history of the world, but there is not one person whose biographers' concentrated analysis overwhelmingly homed in on the events of the final week of their heroes' lives.

We might have expected Paul to write that the word of the cross is the wisdom of God, or the love of God, or the mercy of God, or the grace of God, but he says that the proclamation of the crucifixion is the *power* of God. What God did on Calvary was far more than all that the brilliant achievements of mere man could ever accomplish. The transference of guilt from the souls of an innumerable company of people to the God-man had to entail unimaginable divine energy as well as God's vast mercy. It required omnipotent power, that same love and might that made a cosmos by a divine word. The daily transformation of all who claim, "I was crucified with Christ" can be affected only by omnipotence.

All the evangelical church is wringing its hands about a crisis stemming from a felt lack of power in her pulpits. Christians feel marginalized as their presence and opinions are brushed aside like a fly, ignored by the watching world. There are many suggestions as to how a powerful, living voice from heaven may be heard again in our gatherings, but Paul tells us that this cannot occur apart from the word, the logic, the doctrine of the cross. It is the one declaration that God will always accompany with His power. I do not mean the vain repetition of a phrase like "Jesus died for our sins" but rather a recitation of the rich, multifaceted explanations of what was occurring on the green hill far away that has transformed the destiny of the universe and will continue to change the lives of millions until the end of the world. The professing church will always be quite impotent and powerless without this big declaration of the accomplishments of the Son of God on Golgotha. Rather, the absence of the cross—as it is revealed to us in the New Testament—will always result in a vacuum at the heart of our worship, like Shakespeare's *Hamlet* without the Prince, like van Gogh's paintings without the sunflowers, like the history of American baseball without a mention of Babe Ruth, like the victory of the Second World War without Churchill. Without the cross, the sermon becomes a display of the wisdom of man, a hopelessly insipid collection of religious and moral comments.

There are, alas, core Christian truths that are being ignored in our generation. They are not fertilizing and fructifying the living structures of a congregation, to its enormous detriment and declension. The salt has lost its savor, and thus there is putrefaction. The light is under a bucket, and thus there is darkness.

I will be absolutely honest with you. In these pages I am set on describing to everyone who reads them the Bible's explanation of the cross of Christ. I want to draw men and women to live henceforth, night and day, under the refreshing and life-renewing shadow of Calvary. I do so with some reservations—for example, my own unfitness to write of such an event. Many are wiser and more sensitive than I am. But another concern is that many Christians are already well versed in this subject, and further knowledge might have the

INTRODUCTION

very opposite effect than that great response, "love so amazing, so divine, demands my soul, my life, my all."[1] In other words, I and perhaps some of you could become puffed up and develop a barren familiarity with sacred truth. We might end up suffering from a cool informality with the cross.

That is a calamity for many who know about the "green hill far away."[2] If a Christian asks a child who has always gone to a gospel church why Jesus died on the cross, he will get the prompt answer, "for our sins." Many have learned, since their childhood, about the "wonder-working power in the precious blood of the Lamb."[3] We know it and we sing it, but however much we know, there is still far more to know. But many of us are utterly unthinking about the shocking dilemma that Calvary presents to us.

I ask you to follow me as I make this point, that one day in one place in God's creation, our Creator acted, and God bruised God. The holy, harmless, undefiled Son of God submitted Himself to bear the divine response to sinning; that two millennia ago He hung on the cross and His soul began to experience death, separation from God, the flames of divine wrath, and the pains of hell; that God's magnificent rectitude consumed Christ on a little hill called Golgotha, the place of the skull, the venue for public executions outside the gates of Jerusalem. God was inflicting His Son with all His just and holy revulsion as He focused on cosmic sin. Christ cried out, "My God, My God, why have You forsaken Me?"

---

1. Isaac Watts, "When I Survey the Wondrous Cross," in the public domain.
2. Cecil Frances Alexander, "There Is a Green Hill Far Away," in the public domain.
3. Lewis E. Jones, "Power in the Blood," in the public domain.

(Matt. 27:46). The divine reply was, in effect, "That all the people I gave You, numbered like the sands on the seashore, might not perish but have everlasting life." The Father condemned His Son so that all who are joined to Him might become His eternal children. That is why the Lord Jesus tasted the violent and bloody death of the cross.

What did the death of Christ achieve? The answer is found within Holy Scripture. The apostle Paul takes pains to acknowledge that his own awakening and life-changing ministry came from what he had received from Jesus. Knowledge had been given to him by the exalted and living Christ, explaining to Paul's total satisfaction that He had died for our sins according to the Scriptures and that He was buried and rose again according to the Scriptures. What Paul received was confirmed by all that he had read in the Old Testament Scriptures and by what he had heard from other eyewitnesses of the life, death, and resurrection of Jesus Christ. Paul had been entrusted with this divine and loving gift from God, a rich and clear explanation of the logic of Calvary.

If the supreme end of man is to glorify God, then we must heed what the apostle Paul once wrote: "God forbid that I should boast except in the cross of our Lord Jesus Christ" (Gal. 6:14). The message of the dying love of Jesus Christ is what the church is called to glory in. It is, above every other message in the world, the one that mightily achieves man's chief end of glorifying and enjoying God. We must all know this.

Let us remember the fact that the whole world is confronted day after day with a certain massive historical fact, that the incarnate God, our Creator, was killed through being nailed to a cross—nakedly, publicly, shamefully—outside the city of Jerusalem two millennia ago. As that is a fact of history, doesn't it compel everyone to ask, What's this all about? What's its meaning? What's its significance? What does it have to say to us in the twenty-first century as to what we are to believe and how we are to live? What kind of message are the followers of Jesus Christ to bring to our world? What is to be our explanation of the death of Jesus of Nazareth on a cross, that horrible act of capital punishment at the orders of Gentile and Jew alike and actually confirmed by His Father, who was delivering Him into their cruel hands? The apostles took the message of the cross around the Mediterranean Basin, and that word transformed the lives of many hundreds of thousands of people. It is just as relevant and life-transforming today as it was twenty centuries ago.

In other words, Christianity claims that there is one true understanding of the cross, and it causes a radical response in favored men and women. No other understanding can create that change in thinking and values. No other message contains such extraordinary power. We are claiming that there is but one valid understanding of the crucifixion of Jesus Christ. Of course, it is multiperspectival, but once that understanding has grabbed you, it means that things are never the same again. As a direct consequence, you begin to love God as never before; you love your neighbors quite selflessly, you deny yourselves, husbands love their wives in a certain way, and so on.

A pastor named John Arthur Kingham, who died in 2022, began to see his life and guilt in a new way in the late 1960s, and he carried the burden of his sinfulness month after month. Then these words of an old hymn came to him in a powerful way, and new life began as he delighted for the first time in the means of grace each Sunday and a growing interest in the message of the Scriptures:

> The vilest sinner out of hell,
> Who lives to feel his need,
> Is welcome to a Throne of Grace,
> The Saviour's blood to plead.[4]

Other interpretations of the death of Jesus of Nazareth are impotent and unsatisfying. One interpretation is that His death was a tragedy, another says that He was a pacifist, and still another claims that this was the supreme martyrdom of another brave, reforming prophet. What a valiant young man! The modernists want to give Jesus the Victoria Cross or a Purple Heart. No! Only the message of the cross of Jesus as it is interpreted in the Word of God can change everything, can make things different, can bring down the blessing of God on us and constrain us to give our lives to serving Jesus Christ. All of that is possible when God opens our minds and we are confronted with the Bible's clear message of how Christ's sacrifice on Calvary delivers us from our indifference and ignorance.

You may ask me if I am sure of this. Is it necessary for the world to have this one understanding of Golgotha and to reject any theory that is different? The answer to that hangs entirely on one fact, and that is the true identity of the one hanging on the cross. Jesus alone can interpret His own death—not me, not any man. He supplies the sole authentic understanding of His sacrificial act. For example, the Lord

---

4. William Gadsby, "Glad Tidings," in the public domain.

explained His coming death in these words: "Even the Son of Man did not come to be served, but to serve, and to give His life a ransom for many" (Mark 10:45). And John the Baptist, the herald whom God sent to prepare the people for Christ's public appearance, said, "Behold! The Lamb of God who takes away the sin of the world!" (John 1:29). Christ's apostles, at Pentecost, did not think that His death was a dreadful tragedy. They actually declared that Christ was delivered up to the cross "by the determined purpose and foreknowledge of God" (Acts 2:23), and after Pentecost they explained with increasing clarity and insistence that Jesus died in order to deal with our sins. The early church was in total agreement that the one who died on that cross was our redeeming God and that if we entrust ourselves to Him then He will become our Savior and free us from the guilt of all our sins.

You may ask why it was necessary that the Son of God should die this death. I answer by saying that this is the nature of who and what God is, that without the shedding of blood there is no remission of sin. The wages of sin is always death (Rom. 6:23)—either our death or the penal substitutionary death of God the Son. And it is not just any kind of death, one of old age surrounded by loved ones. Not that. It is one that suffers under the wrath and condemnation of God the Father.

God began to teach this visibly and pictorially during that long Old Testament period, when His followers had a child-like grasp of redemption. During those centuries God set up the temple, the altar, and the sacrifices for sin. The children of Israel were instructed to take spotless lambs from their herds, symbolically placing their hand on the lamb's head, sacrificing the animal, and laying it on the altar as an offering to God for their sins. These prophetic "types" spoke to them of a day when God's great sacrificial Lamb would come from heaven.

During that old dispensation, God sent Moses and the prophets to speak to men and women about the coming Messiah, and throughout those centuries He told them more and more about whom the Anointed One would be—His titles, His virgin birth, where He would be born, and how He would die but rise again.

In the fullness of time, God Himself—God the Son, the Messiah—came into our world. He took on frail flesh by being begotten in the womb of Mary and emerging into the world via the birth canal. Then He grew in stature and wisdom and proceeded to live a life that no man has ever lived before or since. As a young man He bore the just punishment of God and died as no man ever has, and He rose on the third day. His death was not simply the death of a martyr, of a holy man, of a reforming prophet who failed. On that cross hung the one who claimed, "I and My Father are one" (John 10:30), the one whom John claimed was in the beginning with God and was Himself God. Before we go any further, we must know the identity of the man on the cross in all the paradox it brings to us.

> Who is He on yonder tree, dies in grief and agony?
> 'Tis the Lord! O wondrous story!
> 'Tis the Lord! the King of glory![5]

Think of it—the one who is hanging between two evil criminals; the one who submits to the blindfold, the mockery, the beating from soldiers, the crown of thorns, the scourging,

---

5. Benjamin Russell Hanby, "Who Is He in Yonder Stall," in the public domain.

and the sledgehammer nailing hands and feet to the cross; the one who is being killed is the one who, Paul tells us, was "in the form of God" (Phil. 2:6). In other words, the one hanging on that cross is the infinite, eternal, unchangeable, and almighty Creator, Sustainer, and Judge of the world. In this brief statement Paul brings together the atonement and the incarnation. What cruelty, what inhumanity, that our fellow creatures should have treated the loveliest and the best in that way!

> He held the highest place above,
> Adored by all the sons of flame,
> Yet such His self-denying love,
> He laid aside His crown and came
> To seek the lost,
> And at the cost
> Of heavenly rank and earthly fame
> He sought me—Blessed be His name![6]

This creates a dilemma: How can this become a gospel? How can we understand God the Son's crucifixion so that it is turned into good news—indeed, the best of all news? How does the Word of God interpret the cross for us? For the answer to these vital questions, we must go to the divine revelation preserved in Scripture, the all-sufficient and explanatory gift of God to mankind, recorded by those authorized and inspired apostles of Christ. There alone we find the definitive content of biblical Christianity, and there we learn the following truths explaining the reasons for the crucifixion of the Son of God.

---

6. C. A. Tydeman, "I Have a Friend, Whose Faithful Love," in the public domain.

1

REVELATION

We glimpse much of the glory of God through Christ's death.

Golgotha is a revelation of the depravity found in the hearts of men and women—that you and I, under the right circumstances, are capable of doing what no other creature made by God could ever do: nail a man to a cross and let Him hang there in exquisite pain hour after hour, mocking Him as He suffers. And consider who is hanging there. It is gentle Jesus, meek and mild. The man to whom mothers brought their children and placed them in His arms, that He might pray for them. The one whose first words, when they lifted Him up on the cross and dropped it into its socket, were a prayer for His killers: "Father, forgive them, for they do not know what they do" (Luke 23:34). We men nailed the loveliest and the best to a cross. What a revelation of what human depravity is capable of doing.

But something else, something far greater, is revealed on Golgotha. Imagine visiting the bedside of a dying Christian friend, and there you meet a man at peace, full of wisdom and hope, with an anticipation of the heaven that he is confident is shortly to be his eternal destination. What a revelation of the power of the Holy Spirit within this man's life to give him such tranquility and assurance. So, too, when you "survey the wondrous cross on which the Prince of Glory died,"[1] you are also confronted with a divine revelation of the glory of God. What is it that Calvary is clearly declaring? What is its message?

The Holiness of God

What do you find as you consider the cross? The treachery of a disciple, the flight of the eleven, the unjust trial, the place of execution, the brutality, the crucifixion, the mockery, and so on. Is it lovely? Not at all. Calvary is darkness and ugliness. It is all proclaiming one observation to the world: "See man in his sin." Golgotha is ugly because sin is ugly, and we look at the deformity and the cruelty and the anomaly of bringing together the Holy One of God with all of that.

So what does the living God think of sin? How does He deal with it? Does He merely sigh? Does He turn a blind eye? At Calvary you see this marvel: He has chosen to place in the hands of His Son a cup, and the Son takes it. It contains damnation and yet Jesus receives it, for it is impossible for there to be any other cup that He can drink that will save those whom He loves. He takes it and makes it His. And God condemns Him. God turns His face from the one made sin. He forsakes Jesus. The Lord is broken and cursed. And it is all saying to whoever has ears to hear that God does not condone sin, even in His Son when it is imputed to Him. In order to reconcile the world to Himself, that great element of the divine

---

1. Watts, "When I Survey the Wondrous Cross."

righteousness has to be registered. He does not condone what contradicts all that He is and all He stands for. God's absolute integrity is maintained. God will never betray His holiness.

The Love of God
Nothing else in all the world demonstrates God's love for all of us the way Golgotha does, not all the beauty of creation, not all His patience with us, not all His forbearance—nothing surpasses Jesus dying on the cross at Calvary.

> Jesus, my soul, adoring, bends
> To love so full, so free;
> And may I hope that love extends
> Its sacred power to me?[2]

Jesus died for His friends while they were still scornful and utterly indifferent enemies. God purposed that His only Son should die in the place of those who hated Him. He so loved us and repentant sinners all the world over that He did not spare His Son. He was intent on sparing us and redeeming us so that we might go at last to heaven, saved by His precious blood. The infinite, eternal, divine Son of God took on full humanity, made in all points as we are except for our sin. Then He once and for all took responsibility for every speck of our guilt and blame. Bearing the shame and condemnation, the Son of God became the Lamb of God. The holy and blameless Jesus was made sin for us. His atonement is as infinite and eternal and powerful as He is Himself. Who can fathom this? It is more than mortal man can grasp. If God in His love has given us the greatest gift of all—His

---

2. Anne Steele, "And Did the Holy and the Just," in the public domain.

Son—then He will surely give us everything else. Everything means everything. It all comes from the love of God in Jesus Christ.

> Jesus' love is love unbounded,
> Without measure, without end:
> Human thought is here confounded;
> 'Tis too vast to comprehend:
> Praise the Saviour;
> Magnify the sinner's Friend.[3]

The cross is Christ's altar, and it is His throne from which He rules and spoils His enemies, but it is also His pulpit. He speaks to us through Golgotha, and the Holy Spirit opens the ears and hearts of many favored people to hear it. The Spirit sustains the grace of obedience and constantly explains to these blessed sinners the meaning of the cross, and He enables us to plead the blood of the one mediator between God and man, Jesus Christ. So, Father, Son, and Holy Spirit all are engaged in saving us in their love and grace.

The Grace of God

The Father glorifies sinners by removing their guilt and imputing it to His Son, forgiving them for all their sins, joining them to the Lord Christ, indwelling them by His Spirit, and loving them with the very same affection that He displays toward His only begotten Son. That is the achievement of His grace. Rather than sparing His only Son, God

---

3. Thomas Kelly, "Glory, Glory Everlasting Be to Him Who Bore the Cross," in the public domain.

the Father chose to spare many sinners, as numerous as the grains of sand.

Grace is Jesus raising Lazarus from the tomb by commanding one who had been dead for several days to "come forth" (John 11:43). A dead man cannot hear or respond unaided. We are dead in our sins, but the resurrected Christ focuses that same resurrection power on favored sinners, enabling them to hear, understand, believe, and entrust themselves to Himself for pardon and eternal glory. Being born again is not the result of something we can do; it is a sovereign act of God by which we are enabled to appropriate the living Christ by divine grace. The message of the cross is foolishness to us, and it is impossible for us to believe in a crucified God for eternal life until the Spirit of Christ begins to work in our hearts. We cannot come to Jesus unless we are drawn to Him by His grace. We are dead in our sins, but God deals with that by making us alive in Christ. God gives us new birth and strength, and so when we believingly read in Scripture of the power of Jesus Christ crucified, which is far greater than all the powers of sin's temptations, the devil's devices, and the world's enticements, that same power of the cross and the empty tomb becomes active in us to give us eternal life. The fullness of God's redeeming love to us is an act of His grace that delivers us from death through the achievements of Christ's life and death. The conception of the Christian life, its continuance, and its consummation are all through God's grace, which softens our hearts, illuminates our minds, responds in humbling agreement to the Holy Spirit's convicting and assuring work, and plants in us the faith to believe that the Lamb of God has taken away our sin.

All such immense and eternal blessings are the fruit of Calvary, bought for us by Jesus's precious blood. Salvation from beginning to end belongs to the Lord!

The Justice of God

Consider the revelation of God's justice in the sufferings of Christ, the divine judgment that He endured in the place of all believing sinners. When you mark His agonies, you will readily see why Justice is revealed on the hill of Golgotha. Should Justice come to you today saying, "Sinner, you have sinned, and I will punish you," then you know your answer: "Justice, you have already punished all my sins. All I ought to have suffered has been suffered by my substitute, Jesus. It is true that in myself I owe you a debt greater than I can pay, but it is gloriously true that in Christ I owe you nothing whatsoever. For all I once owed has been paid, every penny of it has been cleared, no debt whatsoever remains that is due from me to you, O righteous Justice of God. Guilty and vile though I am, I must prepare always to plead that His bloody sacrifice is enough to satisfy God's demands against me. Oh, yes, I trust I can always plead, 'For Jesus's sake show me mercy!'"

> My faith would lay her hand,
> On that dear head of Thine,
> While like a penitent I stand,
> And there confess my sin.[4]

I find Charles Spurgeon's comments responding to the justice of God revealed on Golgotha very fitting:

---

4. Isaac Watts, "Not All the Blood of Beasts," in the public domain.

Jesus, I believe that thy sufferings were for me; and I believe that they are more than enough to satisfy for all my sins. By faith I cast myself at the foot of thy cross and cling to it. This is my only hope, my shelter, and my shield. It cannot be that God can smite me now. Justice itself prevents, for when Justice once is satisfied it were injustice if it should ask for more. Now, is it not clear enough to the eye of every one, whose soul has been aroused, that Justice stands no longer in the way of the sinner's pardon? God can be just, and yet the justifier. He has punished Christ, why should he punish twice for one offence? Christ has died for all his people's sins, and if thou art in the covenant, thou art one of Christ's people. Damned thou canst not be. Suffer for thy sins thou canst not. Until God can be unjust, and demand two payments for one debt, he cannot destroy the soul for whom Jesus died. "Away goes universal redemption," says one. Yes, away it goes, indeed. I am sure there is nothing about that in the Word of God. A redemption that does not redeem is not worth my preaching, or your hearing, Christ redeemed every soul that is saved; no more, and no less. Every spirit that shall be seen in heaven Christ bought. If he had redeemed those in hell, they never could have come there. He has bought his people with his blood, and they alone shall he bring with him. "But who are they?" says one. Thou art one, if thou believest. Thou art one, if thou repentest of thy sin. If thou wilt now take Christ to be thy all in all, then thou art one of his; for the covenant must prove a lie, and God must be unjust, and justice must become unrighteousness, and love must become cruelty, and the cross must become a fiction, before thou canst be condemned if thou trustest in Jesus.[5]

---

5. Charles Spurgeon, "A Sermon (No. 255) Delivered on Sabbath Morning, May 29th, 1859, by the Rev. C. H. Spurgeon at the Music Hall, Royal Surrey Gardens," Blue Letter Bible, accessed July 15, 2023, https://www.blueletterbible.org/Comm/spurgeon_charles/sermons/0255.cfm.

2

IMPUTATION

God imputed our sin to Christ, and His righteousness to us.

Imagine meeting a happy man, one who strikes you as being at peace with himself, with his neighbors, and with God. He carries no burden of guilt and shame, yet he totally lacks egotism. He rarely talks of himself; there is no self-promotion. In your consideration he is indeed a blessed man, and you wish you could be more like him. Do you know why he is in this state?

We are given the reason in Psalm 32: "Blessed is he whose transgression is forgiven, whose sin is covered. Blessed is the man to whom the LORD does not impute iniquity, and in whose spirit there is no deceit" (vv. 1–2). Imputation is attributing something good or bad to someone, then dealing with that person in the light of that imputation. Allow me to share a brief story with you that illustrates the meaning of this word.

We read in 1 Samuel 22 that, while being hunted by King Saul, David had come to a place called Nob, the city of the priests. A priest called Ahimelech had been kind to him. He had prayed for David, given him food, and provided him with the sword of Goliath. King Saul had heard that the priest had done this, and he summoned all the priests of Nob to come to his palace. The king was very angry with them: "You've been conspiring against me. Why else should you have done all this to assist David? Isn't it that he might rise up against me?" (see v. 13). Ahimelech protested to Saul that no one had been more loyal to him than David, Saul's own son-in-law. The priest said to Saul, "Let not the king impute anything to his servant, or to any in the house of my father. For your servant knew nothing of all this, little or much" (v. 15). Ahimelech says, in effect, "Don't charge him or us with something that is false. What you are saying about David simply isn't true. Please don't impute anything evil to David. He is your loyal subject and a faithful man for whom I pray."

Ahimelech is pleading with Saul not to treat David as a criminal or classify him as an enemy, not to attribute wickedness to him, not to regard him as a rebel. He is a faithful man. Imputation is to attribute something good or bad to someone and then deal with him correspondingly. We can all appreciate the serious consequences of such actions. Someone spreads evil reports about a man of God, that he is an egomaniac, that he always has to have his own way, that he is negligent as a pastor. This accuser is imputing wickedness to a man of God, treating him as if he were an evil man. Such imputation of evil is very painful.

Adam's sin and guilt have been imputed to us because he was our federal head; we were involved in his rebellion against our God, just as we are involved in decisions our prime minister or president makes for our good or ill. We were all in Adam when he defied God, and it is perfectly right for the Lord to treat us as He does. In Adam we all sinned and died.

It is not as though day after day we have to be forced to marginalize and defy God. There's no command from heaven that says to us every morning, "Now, ignore God today. Just think about yourself and please yourself today," and we reluctantly comply. Men and women consistently and freely choose to keep the living God outside of their lives every day.

So Adam's guilt is our guilt, imputed to us. We've gone the way of our father Adam; we share his identical nature. In Adam all die, and we deserve eternal death because we are sinners. That sinful nature is original to us, and so forgiveness is essential, atonement is necessary, new life is required. We need the cross because of what we are. What then is the way that our sins can be removed?

We are supplying some of the biblical insights from a host of perspectives as to why the Lord Jesus had to die. We know at a purely human level one real answer, that it was because of the testimony of false witnesses. They were bribed or threatened or cajoled into imputing wickedness to our Lord. They testified, "We have heard him speak blasphemous words against Moses and God" (Acts 6:11), and blasphemy was a capital offense in theocratic Israel, so He was condemned to be crucified. But virtually everyone in the world's "jury room," with few exceptions, agrees that Jesus was set up; the men were false witnesses. Jesus of Nazareth guilty of blasphemy? The very idea is beyond contempt. What could the preacher of the Sermon on the Mount have done that was worthy of being crucified? What did the man who went about doing good suddenly do to receive such condemnation?

Everything about Jesus was good through and through. His friends who lived with Him for three years compared

Him to a lamb without spot and blemish. They quoted the Scriptures about Him: "[He] committed no sin, nor was deceit found in His mouth" (1 Peter 2:22). In other words, He spoke utterly sincerely in all He said. Pilate's wife said to her husband that he should have nothing to do with killing this man (Matt. 27:19). A criminal dying alongside him said that Jesus had done nothing wrong (Luke 23:41). The centurion who was superintending the execution said that surely He was a righteous man—the Son of God (v. 47). Even God the Father, who knew everything about Jesus, said, "This is My beloved Son, in whom I am well pleased" (Matt. 3:17).

Imagine a special machine that can detect the slightest evidence of sin. You stand the Lord Jesus in front of it and switch it on. When you look at Him through the scrutinizing eyes of this imaginary machine, in His whole being there's not one tiny trace of sin. Not a buzz. Not a flashing light. So here is a man who had lived in an ordinary home with His parents and siblings and who worked with His father in a carpenter's workshop for seventeen or so years. He debated and argued with inquirers and enemies for three years, and yet He remained as holy as God. His meat and drink was to do the will of God. There was never one off guard moment when He came short of the glory of God.

So why did such a blameless man die? Why didn't God protect Him and prevent Him from dying? If some ruffians were torturing your beloved only son, wouldn't you rescue him? Wouldn't even a bad man do that for his son? If you just watched and let him go on suffering terrible pain until they finished him off—and you did nothing when you had the power to save him—wouldn't you be as bad as his killers?

Why didn't God deliver Jesus if He delighted in Jesus? Was there some sin He'd committed? None whatsoever. Then why did His Father permit Him to die like that? Why did God stand back and do nothing? Where's the fair play? Where is the love of God? The Lord delivered Elijah from starvation, Jonah from death in the belly of a whale, Daniel from lions, the three men in Babylon from the furnace's flames, Lazarus from death, the Gadarene demoniac from a legion of demons, Peter from prison, and Paul from drowning. They were all sinners and yet God delivered them, but here is the blessed, sinless Jesus, the Word who was with God and who was God from the beginning, the one whom He calls His "beloved Son," and where is the rescue mission? Why isn't a squadron of angels swooping down in a heavenly commando raid? Why are the hosts of heaven mere spectators of the suffering of their Lord? Why should Jesus endure all of this, or any of this, for longer than a second? He'd done nothing worthy of such an end, yet He was impaled to a cross with the heavens dark above Him. He cried out, "My God, My God, why have You forsaken Me?" (Matt. 27:46).

Why should God add such horrible insult to the injury of the lash and the nails, turning His back on the one He loves the most at His hour of greatest need? Is there knowledge with God of things below? Does the Almighty know what's going on? Yes, He does; He is omniscient. Then the question of questions is why Jesus of Nazareth, the Son of God, should suffer like that under the wrath of a sin-hating God when He is pure and kind, holy and sinless, without a single blemish of character. He loved God with all His heart and soul and mind and strength—the only man ever to have done so. He loved

His neighbor as Himself—the only man ever to have done so. Yet God stood by and watched Jesus suffer such a horrendous and humiliating death. Why? How can the reputation of God Almighty be saved?

It can be saved if you understand this term, *imputation*. In 2 Corinthians 5 the apostle Paul, someone who has been commissioned to go as a herald of Jesus Christ, wrote, "God was in Christ reconciling the world to Himself, not imputing their trespasses to them.... For He made Him who knew no sin to be sin for us, that we might become the righteousness of God in Him" (vv. 19, 21).

Paul is saying something absolutely breathtaking about Golgotha. Something immensely important was accomplished in the agonizing death of Jesus that could not have been achieved otherwise. It was this, that on Calvary, God "made Him who knew no sin to be sin for us." God was there imputing our sin to Christ. We can say it in a dozen ways, but the message is always the same: He was accounting Christ to be a sinner. He was charging Jesus with our guilt. He was ascribing to the spotless Son the shame and blame of our bad behavior. In our place God the Son was being condemned. The Father was making His Son answer for our wrongdoing, and Jesus freely chose to be made sin for us because He loved us so much and was taking our place so that we might be redeemed. The Father and the Son were in harmonious agreement that because of their great mutual and eternal love for us this could be the only way that we fallen sons of Adam most certainly will be redeemed. Something in the very nature of God requires that death inevitably has to be the wages of sin. Without the shedding of blood there can be no remission. That is how God is. So let me break it down. What do we see on Golgotha?

The apostle Paul declares to us these truths:

- On the cross the innocence of Christ was being confirmed.
- On the cross the wonderful loving-kindness and grace of God was being revealed.
- On the cross the sins of repenting believers were imputed to the Lord Jesus.
- On the cross God's righteousness was satisfied.

That is the good news that Calvary proclaims. I plead with you to let the truth of the imputation of your sins to Christ be the whole truth about the way things are between you and God today. There is no barrier whatsoever; there is no impediment; there is no closed or limited access. It has all been forgiven; it is remembered no more.

I am affirming the message of the cross, that the sins of all the people of God, as many people as the stars in the heavens, have all been imputed to the Lord Christ and forgiven. He has borne them all: every speck, every spot, every such thing has been imputed to Christ there. There is absolutely nothing left. The single determinant today of your relationship with God is what happened on the cross. Nothing else matters; nothing else is relevant. There are only two factors in the equation: what God did and how Christ responded. God made Christ sin, and He received all that guilt lovingly. And how you feel about your life, how sometimes you doubt, and how you fail are not remotely relevant to Golgotha. The one thing that matters is that God made Christ to be sin. And I don't for a moment believe that the heart which knows that will take advantage of it and go from this understanding of our sins to continue in drunkenness or stealing or deceiving or living a life of lawlessness—the cross simply won't let you!

I believe, on the contrary, that if imputation has no place in your thinking, if you are living your life with scarcely the smallest consideration of what Jesus Christ did for you on Golgotha, and if you are still feeling that God has things against you, it may indicate some unconscious grudge against God that somehow is used to justify you from being less than perfect. It permits a relapse here and a shortcoming there. But I want you to know in the depths of your heart that when God made Jesus Christ sin for us, our Savior made a proper job of that sin, that He dealt with it all 100 percent, that He cleared it all away, that He experienced its hell in your place, that He entered its outer darkness instead of you so that you shall never, never know the inextinguishable fires of hell. When God comes to you searching for your sin, He will discover it on the cross of Jesus, condemned there and covered, and on that fact is your whole confidence of forgiveness grounded.

Christ has died, yet men may perish; full atonement has been made, but many are on the broad road heading for destruction; the sinless one has been made sin, but still men die without hope and without God; the full gospel has been preached, but many still reject it. So I implore you not to refuse, not to harden your hearts. I beseech you in the light of eternity, in the name of a sin-hating God, in the certainty of death, in the light of the arms of love stretched out to you, be reconciled to God. Why should this estrangement between God and you go on any longer? Do not put down this book unreconciled! Do not take your sin and guilt away with you. The Son of God is prepared to take your guilt and blame. I plead with you to take advantage of God's mercy. Entrust yourself to Jesus Christ. Receive Him into your life. From now on walk with Him, live for Him, trust in Him, flee from all your sins, flee from all your good works, hide in His wounded side. Jesus will receive sinners; He will receive you. Do not reject Him. I assure you today that if you are reconciled to Him, life will be yours, pardon will be yours, heaven will be yours, all things working together for your good will be yours, a living shepherd never leaving you will be yours, all your needs being richly supplied will henceforth be yours! Who could refuse such an offer? Take Him now as He is freely offered to you in the gospel, and through Him be reconciled to God.

3

HUMILIATION

*The cross of Christ is the most glorious
example of self-humbling.*

In the letter to the Christians in Philippi, Paul is dealing in part with a personality clash between two of the leading women in the congregation. Each knew her experience, years of service, rank, and the respect that she merited. Paul's typical pastoral approach to the estrangement between the two was to bring the greatest theological realities to bear on such basic moral, social, and family duties. He addresses the tensions between those two leading women by reminding them that if any person in the world knew His rank and the respect that was due to Him, it was the Son of God. But He humbled Himself, becoming obedient to death, even death on a cross. Paul tells the women to pour contempt on their pride and to get on with serving the body of Christ and to keep the Lord Jesus's example constantly before them.

We as Christians are confronted with the example of the self-humbling of Christ, the one who has presented to us His example in order that we should walk in His steps. He once left the glories of heaven and the adoration of an innumerable company of angels. He waved goodbye to much of that when He became incarnate. What humiliation!

You turn over a clod of earth and notice a wriggling worm. Imagine you yourself turning into and becoming such a lowly creature! But the gulf between God and man is unimaginably vaster than that between man and worm. The infinite became finite. The unchangeable changed. The omnipresent became located in one place. The immeasurable entered a virgin's womb. The omnipotent became weak. The eternal entered time and became subject to it. The sustainer of all things became dependent, lying in His mother's lap. The omniscient grew in wisdom. While remaining totally divine, the Son of God added full manhood to His deity, sin excepted. What humility!

He spent His first thirty years in a hamlet called Nazareth, where His father was the local carpenter, making doors, fences, posts, chairs, cupboards, and tables. Jesus had designed the atom and had made each galaxy and its billions of star systems. Without Him was not anything made that was made, and yet He worked as a carpenter's assistant! He shared a home with His half brothers and half sisters, sitting at the table with them, listening to and engaging in their chatter, eating the plainest food, sharing a common toilet and a bedroom with the boys. This one had eternally known fellowship with the Father and the Holy Spirit and the adoration of an innumerable company of angels. What humility!

Then He began His ministry, making Himself accessible to everyone day after day. Even on the Sabbath people came to Him needing healing. No days off. There were times when He needed to get up a great while before daybreak and climb up the slopes of a hill to a secret place to have some time alone with His Father. He chose ordinary men to be with Him, teenagers for the most part, lads who did not understand His identity or His mission. They did not comprehend His teaching about the kingdom of God and how it was necessary for Him to suffer in order to establish it. They sought to deflect Him from His appointed pilgrimage. He was forgiving and patient, but they responded to the privileges of hearing Him preach, seeing Him delivering people from satanic dominion, and raising the dead by abandoning Him when soldiers came to arrest Him. But He did not abandon them; He recommissioned them after His resurrection and blessed their ministries for the rest of their lives, always with them. What humility!

The Son of God had conceived of and created iron ore, trees, coal, the gifts of craftsmanship, the spirit of justice, and the righteous punishment of evildoers. But men and women used all that material, skill, and conviction to put the Lord Himself on trial. They even bribed men to tell lies under oath about His alleged blasphemy. Then they took an iron hammer and nails and led Jesus to be executed on a wooden cross that their carpenters had made.

It is often pointed out that there is no description of physical death by crucifixion in the New Testament, but that is surely because it was an all-too-familiar scene to a first-century audience. It could even be found just outside the walls of Jerusalem (crucifixion was hated by the Jews as something cursed); any Jewish traveler might turn a bend in the road and come upon a crucifix with a corpse of a man nailed up there, the vultures tearing off his flesh. They knew what crucifixion was from their experience of a groaning world.

Crucifixion as a punishment was widespread in the ancient world. It was developed around the fifth century BC and was a cheap and cruel punishment that served as the strongest of deterrents to would-be rebels. The upright wooden cross was the most common technique, and the time it took for victims to die would depend on how they were crucified. Those accused of robbery could be tied to the crucifix and, because they could better support their weight with their arms, might survive for several days. Seven-inch nails would be hammered through hands or even a man's wrists so that the arm bones there could support the body's weight. The nail would sever the median nerve, which not only caused immense pain but also paralyzed the victim's hands.

The feet were nailed to the upright part of the crucifix so that the knees were bent at around 45 degrees. But this little platform seems to have been a later feature emerging in the century after our Lord's death. To speed death, executioners would often break the legs of their victims to give them no chance of using their thigh muscles as a support. Once the legs gave out, the weight would be transferred to the arms, gradually dragging the shoulders from their sockets. The elbows and wrists would follow a few minutes later; by now, the arms would be six or seven inches longer. The victim would have no choice but to bear his weight on his chest. He would immediately have trouble breathing as the weight caused the rib cage to lift up and force him into an almost perpetual state of inhalation.

Suffocation would usually follow, but the relief of death could also arrive in other ways. The resultant lack of oxygen in the blood would cause damage to tissues and blood vessels, allowing fluid to diffuse out of the blood into tissues, including the lungs and the sac around the heart. This would make the lungs stiffer and make breathing even more difficult, and the pressure around the heart would impair its pumping. That was death by crucifixion.

Paul writes that Christ died "even the death of the cross" (Phil. 2:8) because he and his readers knew that shameful crucifixion was a punishment reserved for particular kinds of criminals and dissidents. Simple or common crimes such as rape, thievery, or even murder were not often met with crucifixion. Instead, those who were considered a threat to the Pax Romana were most commonly assigned this heinous punishment. Men considered agitators of greater unrest—like slaves, pirates, political rebels, and religious agitators in particular— were criminalized as worthy of this death. The Roman Empire made an example of these criminals as a warning not to stir up the people.

However, the empire considered it distasteful to administer such an awful punishment to full-fledged Roman citizens. In fact, it was seen as a perversion of justice to crucify a citizen in good standing. This punishment was meted out against those who were outside the membership of society.

Cicero spoke strongly against crucifixion, calling it "a most cruel and disgusting punishment." He also said, "The very mention of the cross should be far removed not only from a Roman citizen's body, but from his mind, his eyes, his ears. It is a crime to bind a Roman citizen; to scourge him is a wickedness; to put him to death is almost parricide. What shall I say of crucifying him? So guilty an action cannot by any possibility be adequately expressed by any name bad enough for it."[1]

But the Son of God, out of love for the sinners whom He had been entrusted with, humbled Himself by submitting to this unspeakably horrible punishment, so shameful, agonizingly cruel, and violent.

The apostle Paul, a Roman citizen, was protected by law from such a death, but the Lord Jesus Christ could not and would not make any attempt to escape from it. He had come to do His Father's will with great delight. He came as a servant subject to His Master. He came in love for the people His Father had given to Him, whom He was determined to save from destruction.

> When on the cross, my Lord I see
> Bleeding to death, for wretched me;
> Satan and sin no more can move,
> For I am all transformed to love.
>
> His thorns and nails pierce through my heart,
> In every groan I bear a part;
> I view His wounds with streaming eyes,
> But see! He bows His head and dies![2]

So the Son of God submitted Himself to that tearing apart of body and soul, by means of crucifixion, in order to remove the curse from us and provide salvation for all those He loves. That divine love was the great reason Jesus permitted the nails, and the judgment, and the taste of death. For

---

1. Michael Licona, *The Resurrection of Christ: A New Historiographical Approach* (Downers Grove, Ill.: InterVarsity Press, 2010), 304.

2. John Newton, "When on the Cross, My Lord I See," in the public domain.

all His people the Lord Jesus offered Himself—His body, His blood, His sufferings, and His obedience. No one else has ever been good enough to pay the price of sin. None other has ever loved God with all his heart all through his life. The psalmist asks and answers this question, "Who may ascend into the hill of the LORD? Or who may stand in His holy place? He who has clean hands and a pure heart, who has not lifted up his soul to an idol, nor sworn deceitfully" (Ps. 24:3–4). Jesus only! By His life and every minute of His dying could He ascend the hill of the Lord and sit down at the right hand of God.

The apostle thus makes a staggering conclusion when he tells the church in Philippi and thus every single Christian to "let this mind be in you which was also in Christ Jesus" (Phil. 2:5). He is telling us to think and act just like the Son of God. And so that is the sincere desire of everyone who is spiritually joined to Him. For example, when the deacon Stephen was being stoned to death, he cried to God, as his Lord had done, on behalf of his tormentors, "Lord, do not charge them with this sin" (Acts 7:60). The cross is the power of God to sanctify all who have died in Christ. They are utterly dead to their former lifestyle or acting as everyone else behaves. Those who have died in Christ and trust Him as their Lord and Savior cannot act like that. Calvary will not allow it!

> His dying crimson like a robe,
> Spreads o'er his body on the Tree;
> Then am I dead to all the globe,
> And all the globe is dead to me.[3]

---

3. Watts, "When I Survey the Wondrous Cross."

4

RETRIBUTION

The cross was the Lord Jesus Christ being penalized.

Some deaths seem to be utterly meaningless exhibitions of cruelty, such as the killing of children in a school massacre. The grieving parents all say, "What was the point? Why kill them? They'd done that fellow no harm. He didn't know one of them. It is unbelievably cruel and meaningless."

Golgotha was not a meaningless event to the people of Jerusalem. They knew why capital punishment had been visited upon all three of those crucified men at the Place of the Skull. They had criminalized our Lord Jesus, sending soldiers armed with swords and clubs and torches to arrest Him. They had conducted a number of trials in various courts of law. Then they mocked and beat up the Son of God. He was put on trial before the high priests and the Sanhedrin, where bribed witnesses said that they had heard Him blaspheme. He was tried before Pilate and Herod, the representatives of the governing Roman authority. His alleged crimes were blasphemy and making Himself a king in the Roman Empire. Those trials all resulted in the same verdict: "Guilty!" And so they sentenced Him to be crucified to death. On all those crosses, on what we today call Good Friday, penalties were being paid, and those criminals who had been sentenced endured a terrible death.

This is the beginning of a factual understanding of Calvary. It was in the eyes of the governing authorities retribution for Jesus's crimes. He was paying a penalty for wrongdoing, and the penalty was His life. We all know what a penalty is, whatever little you know of some sport or other. When rules of the sport are broken, a punishment is administered by a referee, the man in charge. A penalty is the result of wrongdoing, a response to law breaking. In our daily lives car owners are penalized for all kinds of driving offenses, for parking in a forbidden zone, for driving in a bus lane, for exceeding the speed limit. Then they pay a penalty charge. Even children in school are punished for breaking school rules.

The New Testament takes that fundamental category, the very familiar idea that wrongdoing brings upon the culprit some penalty or other, and uses it as an explanation of what was happening to the Son of God on Golgotha. Jesus of Nazareth was being tried for blasphemy and for challenging the sole authority of Caesar by claiming to be a king. This was a capital offense. He was found guilty, and the penalty was being sentenced to death by the cross.

But there is another penalty being paid on Golgotha, and it is not the penalty demanded by human beings. It is the penalty that God requires. Who has been sentenced to death by crucifixion? The one who claimed to be in a special relationship with God, saying, "I and My Father are one" (John 10:30). He openly acknowledged that God was His Father, making Himself equal to God. What, then, is happening here? Men are torturing God's Son to death? Yes, this is so. God the Father knew the monstrosity of men's injustice toward Jesus, but He didn't send a legion of angels to rescue Him.

So to a definite degree God was privy to the punishment of His dear Son. God had once rescued Jesus after He had been preaching controversially in the synagogue in Nazareth, making what appeared to the elders of that synagogue blasphemous claims about Himself. Its leaders wanted to throw our Lord off a precipice for what He had said, but Jesus somehow simply slipped away. His Father delivered Him, and the synagogue leaders who wanted Jesus dead couldn't find Him. They weren't able to lay a finger on Him then. But on Golgotha the Father did nothing to spare Him. In fact, it was the very reverse—it was God who "delivered Him up" (Rom. 8:32). God Himself was actually handing Jesus over to His merciless enemies (Acts 2:23). Are we utterly unthinking about the shocking dilemma that Calvary presents to us? On one day in one place on this planet, God bruised God. The holy, harmless, undefiled Son of God submitted Himself to accept and endure the divine response to sin. When He hung on the cross, His soul began to experience death, separation from God, the flames of divine wrath, the pains of hell. God was inflicting His Son with all His just and holy revulsion at sin. Christ cried out, "My God, My God, why have You forsaken Me?" (Matt. 27:46). The divine reply would have been, "In order that all the people I gave You, numbered as many as the sands on the seashore, might not perish but have everlasting life." That is why the Lord Jesus tasted the violent and bloody death of the cross.

Let's stop and give weight to this extraordinary reality, that what we are confronted with at Golgotha is God the Father ultimately penalizing His Son. He did not spare Him from any physical, mental, spiritual, or social agony. He gave Him no analgesic in the body He prepared for Him. Jesus took no myrrh and rough wine to kill the pain and dull His senses. I am challenging you as to whether you have ever considered the appalling problems that such facts create, that the Son of God was actually dying by the determinate counsel and foreknowledge of God His Father. How can that be? Isaiah 53:10 says, "It pleased the LORD to bruise Him." Here is God forsaken by God, stricken by Him and afflicted. The Lord lifted up His rod and it fell on Christ. God punished Christ fully and did not spare Him. Consider the force of a divine punishment and the figure who was its recipient.

What an enormous problem! What could motivate God as He bruises the one of whom He declares, "This is My beloved Son, in whom I am well pleased" (Matt. 3:17)? We must know! Let us interrogate the possible answers.

Was it capriciousness? If so, then what is God going to do next? What new horrors will He choose to do without explanation? Why is God toying with His Son, trifling with His only begotten Son? Was He just in a bad mood? That is utterly unacceptable. God is the ever-blessed Lord. And God is love. There is not one loveless molecule in God. God is not capricious. He is eternal affection, especially for His only Son.

Then was it malice? Is He tormenting His Son maliciously and sadistically? Again, that is an absolutely intolerable explanation. Jesus was always His beloved, and never did the

Father love Him more than when He was humbling Himself to accept the death of the cross. He was the eternal Beloved One throughout the bruising and the forsaking. In what measureless affection the Father held His Son! No, the Father's motivation was not malice or caprice.

Then there is just one remaining interpretation. *This is the holy justice of God*, the anger of God toward everything that contradicts and scorns His loving-kindness, patience, mercy, and divine righteousness. God hates all that is vile. He recoils against it. He does not merely shrug and look the other way. He does not watch the folly of men and women with a hidden smile on His face the way a Buddha appears to! He is not indifferent to the horrors mankind perpetrates against his fellow man. God is light, and in Him there is no darkness *at all*. In God there is always a holy integrity, an absolute inability to condone wickedness.

This alone explains how God the Father could have forsaken His Son at His hour of greatest need. There are great New Testament sayings that shine light on dark Calvary. We discover that "the Lamb of God...takes away the sin of the world" (John 1:29). And the apostle defines for us "the world" in these words: "the lust of the flesh, the lust of the eyes, and the pride of life" (1 John 2:16). On Golgotha it is all being heavily borne on the dying Jesus. We are even told that He was made a curse for those who are justly cursed because of their abhorrent iniquities (Gal. 3:13). We are told that Christ was made sin for sinning men and women (2 Cor. 5:21). In other words, we are being told repeatedly that on Golgotha, Jesus was paying the penalty for iniquitous living. That is simply a fact!

> Who is this that hangs there dying
> While the cruel world scoffs and scorns,
> Numbered with the malefactors
> Torn with nails, and crowned with thorns?
> 'Tis our God, who lives for ever
> 'Mid the shining ones on high,
> In the glorious golden city,
> Reigning everlastingly.[1]

Man will never see the meaning of Golgotha unless he starts there in its breathtaking glory and in its hope and deliverance. Christ was wrongly penalized by Jew and Gentile. He was crucified through the wicked hands of evil weaklings. He was crucified through the determinate council and foreknowledge of God. Both penalized our Lord. Both divine sovereignty and human responsibility are at work in the crucifixion.

So the word of the cross is this: Golgotha was retribution, and Christ paid the penalty of our wickedness. The Lord Jesus had accepted His divinely appointed mission as the sent one who came from heaven to redeem all whom He had been given by His Father. There exists a great aphorism, "Whatever God determines in eternity, men will choose in time." Christ was the Lamb slain "from the foundation of the world" (Rev. 13:8). His mission was to come and receive the just penalty that all of our sinning demands.

Before you were born, before you had done any good or evil, God had planned the salvation of an incalculably vast company of people, as numerous as the grains of sand on the

---

1. William Walsham How, "Who Is This, So Weak and Helpless," in the public domain.

seashore. God saved them all by the life and active obedience of the one mediator, the man Christ Jesus; then, by His death, He submitted Himself to the judgment that was facing them.

The Christian life is not about doing your best to keep all of God's commandments and then being saved and taken to heaven as a reward for your obedience. You and I were not rescued from our bondage to sin and ego and indifference to Christ by our own power and attainments. We are saved by the power that flows from the cross of Jesus. This work is accomplished by the triune God alone. He destroyed the power of Satan. He brought us to hear the gospel. He opened our hearts to receive it. He brought us into the company of faithful Christians to strengthen us and keep us believing the gospel.

You may have hesitated about confessing with your lips that henceforth you are going to be a Christian, because you think, "Ah! I will never be able to live the Christian life. How can I possibly obey God from one day to the next?" I say to you that it is His love and the power displayed on Calvary that will help you in this new life by making you a new person, with new graces, new abilities, and new energy. That new life will be an expression of your gratitude to the Lord for saving you. That thanksgiving will be assisting you to elevate your life. You will live a different life, and you will seek each day to do so by the help of the Holy Spirit. You will live a different life because of the fact that the blood of Jesus Christ, God's Son, has cleansed you from all your guilt. He has been so kind to you that from now on you are overwhelmed with gratitude for all He has done.

> And Thou hast brought to me
> Down from thy home above

> Salvation full and free,
> Thy pardon and thy love;
> Great gifts, great gifts thou broughtest me;
> What have I brought to thee?
>
> O let my life be giv'n,
> My years for thee be spent;
> World-fetters all be riv'n,
> And joy with suff'ring blent:
> Thou gav'st, thou gav'st thyself for me,
> I give myself to thee.[2]

Are you with me? I am addressing your way of thinking. I have more to say by way of explanation of this most glorious and mysterious of events that has ever occurred on our planet. Let me go on…

---

2. Frances Ridley Havergal, "What Have I Given?," in the public domain.

5

SUBSTITUTION

Golgotha was where the Lord Jesus Christ died in our place.

The concept of substitution is neither unusual nor difficult to grasp. We are all aware of what a substitute is. A player is summoned off the bench and takes the place of someone else. On the cross the Son of God paid the penalty of sin, but not for His own wickedness—not for what He had done—for He had no wickedness at all in action, word, imagination, or desire. He was dying as a substitute for all those sinners whom God had given to Him, whom God had sent Him into the world to save.

There is a useful term that can be employed here, and it's the word *vicarious*, meaning "in the place of." I have said that the Lord Jesus's death was retribution, and now I am saying that it was also vicarious, that there was a penal substitution taking place on Calvary. Consider the purity and innocence of the Lord Jesus, His absolute integrity. God Himself was always pleased with Him, every minute of every single day. He never had to overlook His Son's bad behavior or find an excuse for anything He did, the way we try to put our children's misbehavior in the best possible light. Jesus had absolute and happy perfection in His body and mind and affections and imagination. Though tempted in all points as we are, He didn't lick His lips and savor the taste of a single sin. He resisted every temptation. There was never one trespass of His own for which He needed to make atonement.

Now, Jesus's life was not hidden away in a corner. It was a transparent public life lived under constant pressure, under many demands every hour, scrutinized by His enemies, challenged by His mother and the family He loved, misunderstood by His own disciples, being constantly besieged for help night and day. But even Pilate, speaking on behalf of many non-disciples, said this about Jesus: "I find no fault in this Man" (Luke 23:4). The Lord Jesus could humbly challenge His accusers, "Which of you convicts Me of sin?" (John 8:46). One of the criminals dying alongside Him on his cross said to another criminal, "This Man has done nothing wrong" (Luke 23:41). The disciples who lived in His presence for three years, observing everything that this unusual man did, concluded unanimously that He was one who had never said or done anything at all sinful. He was holy, harmless, and undefiled, unlike them. He was not just another sinner who was better than others; not at all. He was rather like a lamb without one single spot or the tiniest blemish.

So here you have this innocent man of total integrity, and it is He who suffers retribution for wrongdoing. He is sinless and yet He is condemned to a criminal's death on a cross. He deserved the honor that God Himself bestowed on His loving, obedient Son in eternity past. He should have been spared the cross and been vindicated, but He was not.

God was totally pleased with His Son, but He did not spare Him. Why? He could have, but God refused.

What we are seeing in Christ on the cross is the ugliness of human wickedness being united to the beauty of our Lord's character. I am not asking you merely to theorize about this. I want you to feel how anomalous that is. I want you to consider the perplexity of this historic fact. This is Jesus, the Prince of Glory. He is dying by being nailed to a cross, and God is not sparing Him. This is the one who made us and everything else there is. This is the infinite, eternal, and unchangeable God who is, by the word of His power, upholding all things—the atom, gravity, the revolving world, the tides, the winds, the moon waxing and waning, and all of us living and moving and having our being in Him. He is the one who is sustaining all of that and infinitely, unimaginably more. Everything in the cosmos keeps going by Christ's will. And yet it is to this divine Lord, the Creator and Sustainer of all things, that the wages of sin—death—are being imputed; they are being laid to His charge, and He is receiving the just condemnation they merit.

I want you to think, *Can it be? What right does God have to bruise His beloved, innocent Son? How can He maintain His integrity and do such a thing?* This also caused much grief to the early church. Cleopas on the road to Emmaus couldn't stop talking about it (Luke 24:18–24). All his hopes had vanished that Jesus of Nazareth was truly the redeemer of God's people. "I'd thought He was the one who would redeem Israel, but now I fear that's quite impossible. God would never have allowed His Anointed to die in such shame and agony." That the Lord Jesus was being punished canceled out the disciples' entire understanding of Him. Cleopas concluded, as did almost all the early doubting church before Pentecost, that Jesus couldn't have been the sinless one loved by God the Father, for God would never have permitted such a monstrosity. It was quite impossible for Cleopas to conceive that God's Anointed had been crucified between two criminals, had been unable to save Himself from the death of the cross, and had not been delivered from it by the power of His Father.

What was Cleopas failing to consider? He had not grasped the meaning of one word, *for*. It is a word you meet in Scripture again and again: "Christ has…become a curse for us" (Gal. 3:13), "Christ died for our sins" (1 Cor. 15:3), "Christ…loved me and gave Himself for me" (Gal. 2:20). Of course, He had also loved God with all His heart and soul for us, He was tempted for us, He cast out demons for us, He fulfilled all righteousness and lived obediently to the will of God for thirty years for us. And if we are going to understand the word of the cross, then we must grasp the significance of the word *for*. What possible meaning can this word have?

There is a *for* of invitation. The servants of the King went into the highways and the hedgerows to announce the invitation the King had made, that anyone who heard His heralds should come to the wedding feast of His Son. "This invitation is for you! Come! You must come!" said His servants. And regarding the death of His Son, His servants are saying to all who have ears to hear, "This sacrifice is for you to take; this blood is for you to be washed in; this atonement has been achieved to cover you!" But this *for* does not only indicate an offer; it also signifies a substitution, that in the place of condemned sinners, the Lamb of God bore the curse that hung over them. In other words, as their substitute He absorbed it, He received it in His own body and soul, He bore it in such a way that they shall never bear it. He drank the cup of damnation to the dregs—that very cup that they should have drunk. Not one drop is left for the guilty ones to taste. They are not being asked, "Please finish off the cup of divine wrath." No! He has left nothing for others to deal with. For all who benefit from what Christ did, there is no condemnation whatsoever. Divine retribution has been satisfied completely by Christ.

> He took the dying traitor's place,
> And suffered in his stead:
> For sinful man—oh wondrous grace!
> For sinful man he bled.[1]

So we are considering this little word *for* in the sense of substitution. Christ lived for us; He loved God for us; He loved His neighbor as Himself for us; He kept the law for us; He resisted temptation for us; He suffered the penalty that sin demanded for us; He was condemned in our place and made a full payment for us.

Consider that marvelous concept the apostle Paul wrote about when he says that Christ is married to His people (Eph. 5:25–32). Our Lord takes all the liabilities of His bride. He is there to clear all her debts, defend her reputation, answer for all her follies, receive her retribution. From that very moment in the beginning when His Father gave Him the hand of His people as His bride, He was eternally joined to them. From

---

1. Anne Steele, "The Wonders of Redemption," in the public domain.

that moment on He has had an everlasting affection for them. They are precious to Him. The Son of God joyfully receives them, embraces them, and holds them to His heart, never letting them go, whatever they've done. The relationship is one of affection: "I am doing this by Myself for My people. I am dying on a cross because I love them." They are on His heart, written there in marks of indelible grace, as He was hanging on the cross all those long hours of darkness. I scarcely can accept it, that He was loving me while nailed there, giving Himself for me! We rejoice before God in the consequent glory of Jesus's great achievement, that because He knew abandonment, we shall never know it. Today we are looking forward to a coming marriage celebration! All is ready, and when we respond to the invitation, we discover that we are to attend a celebratory heavenly feast not as necessary guests but as the bride of the Son of God!

> From heav'n He came and sought her
> To be His holy bride;
> With His own blood He bought her,
> And for her life He died.[2]

We must remember that truth whenever we experience days of darkness. In those moments His voice is saying to us, "I was on the cross. I was making atonement for your sins. There is no retribution for you. God is satisfied. Hear His loving voice and cry out to your Father." We must learn that in all things, at all times, we are still to give thanks to God and express our gratitude to Him: "Lord, spiritually, I am down in the dumps. My heart is cold; I feel lifeless. At my best I am

---

2. S. J. Stone, "The Church's One Foundation," in the public domain.

lukewarm, but I know this, that I can always give You thanks for one thing, for *where I'm not*. And for *what* I'm not. Jesus was made sin that I might be made righteousness in Him. I am not this day under Your frown and contempt, because You, my Lord, exhausted that judgment." The Lord Christ hung hour after hour in the naked flame of the righteousness of God, and the consequence is that my walk is in green pastures, and I will ever be refreshed by the still waters.

So here in the word *for* is substitution—Christ in our place, bearing the fair retribution of that holy law that we have broken, in order that we might be delivered from its judgments and know the blessedness of adoption. That is the essence of biblical Christianity. A biblical Christian is someone who believes in the penal substitutionary death of the Lord Jesus. That is the essence and the foundation of their chief joy. God has displayed to the world how He can remain just and a hater of sin and yet can forgive the wickedness of the worst of men and women. All our law breaking in act and word and feeling and imagination—past, present, and future—has all been condemned in the penal substitutionary sacrifice of His Son on Golgotha.

> In peace let me resign my breath
> And Thy salvation see;
> My sins deserve eternal death,
> But Jesus died for me.[3]

I am urging you to understand why Jesus endured our retribution as our substitute. He took our place so that there

---

3. See "Christ's Vicarious Death," Bible Hub, accessed September 20, 2023, https://biblehub.com/sermons/pub/christ's_vicarious_death.htm.

is now no condemnation to those who are joined by faith to Him. Jesus is the name of the only one who was able to accomplish this. No other religious person had the authority or the power to do this. That means if you want freedom and closeness to God, you must plead the name of Jesus. You must say, "For Jesus's sake forgive me. For Jesus's sake, Father, make me Your child. For Jesus's sake take me to heaven one day. Become my Savior!" And go on praying like that until you know through an inward witness of the Holy Spirit that God has saved you and that your sins—all of them—have been pardoned. Tell it to God. Tell it now, and never stop until you know He has heard you. Then you can say these words of trust:

> He took my sins and my sorrows,
> He made them his very own;
> He bore the burden to Calvary,
> And suffered and died alone.[4]

---

4. Charles H. Gabriel, "I Stand Amazed in the Presence," in the public domain.

6

PROPITIATION

The cross was where the Lord Christ appeased God's wrath.

Propitiation. Now, what does that word mean? It is not some theologian's word that makes things more complicated. Not at all! The very reverse. It is a Holy Spirit word, a Bible word, and so an essential word. It is part of growing in usefulness and maturing as a Christian to understand and use God's words correctly. Consider a teenager who loves motorbikes. When he is with other bikers, he does not talk of this "doohickey" on the engine and that "little black thingy." He takes pleasure in using the correct words. He displays his seriousness about something he loves and wants to master.

So it is with us. This word *propitiation* is found in two places in the New Testament. Paul uses it in Romans 3:25: "Whom God set forth as a propitiation by His blood, through faith, to demonstrate His righteousness, because in His forbearance God had passed over the sins that were previously committed." The apostle John is also inspired to use it in 1 John 2:2: "And He Himself is the propitiation for our sins, and not for ours only but also for the whole world." So we are given a specific word to understand, explain, and use when we are considering the meaning of the cross.

What does *propitiation* mean? By employing that exact noun, both of those apostles were seeking to impress on us one great reality, the effect of the cross upon God. The cross work of Christ is as our substitute and it is also targeting the holy wrath of God. In the book of Psalms we are plainly and unmistakably told of a very sobering reality, that "God is angry with the wicked every day" (7:11). God is angry with each and every one of us for what we have done wrong, yet He continues to love what He has made. He loves the nature He has created, but what fills Him most with wrath toward mankind are the sins that we commit against Him. There is in the holy God a sustained revulsion and indignation against wickedness and man's abhorrent cruelties. He sees the terror-stricken and hears the shrieks, sobs, and screams for help. The God who is light is moved to holy retribution. He watches men burning alive other men, sees child abuse, wife abuse, animal abuse, our tortures, our thefts, our scams, our selling drugs, our kidnappings and abductions, our drunken driving, our racism, our injustices, our pornographies, our false religions.

The world is groaning, and God doesn't say, "Well…I'll just look the other way. I'll just forget about it all." He cannot! He forgets nothing. All things are naked and open to Him, always. Could God shrug His shoulders and look away? He's not callous! All such things make Him burn with holy indignation against all that is tawdry, mean, unspeakable, and unimaginably filled with horror.

Our heavenly Father is not an aloof God. He is not indifferent. He cares! His wrath homes in from heaven against such wickedness and against the people who choose to do such monstrous things—people like me and like you. The God who is light, in whom is no darkness at all, is angry with the wicked every day.

So look again and survey the wondrous cross and see what has happened on Golgotha! There the Son of God dealt with that response of the wrath of Father, Son, and Holy Spirit as they focused with anger on mankind's wickedness. That is the just rectitude of a sin-hating God. There existed in common speech in New Testament times a familiar pagan word that meant "appeasement," and it was used to assure the pagan idol-worshiper of the imagined effect of his sacrifices. "You are now okay. The temple god is content with you," the priestesses would affirm, having received a good payment. The animals' deaths were considered to be sacrifices of propitiation. The New Testament quite deliberately chooses that word to explain the divine impact of Christ's enduring the punishment of sin. It announces that our Lord Jesus has effectively satisfied the wrath of a sin-hating God for all whose hope is in Him.

I am saying that between man and God there is alienation, and this is not simply because of our sins but also because of God's righteous indignation against our misunderstandings, our suspicions of God, our weakness, our ignorance, our errors, our omissions, our unbelief, our cold hearts, our hypocrisy. We need to understand the solemnity of His infinite integrity and wrath that must be dealt with. He does not condone; He does not tolerate; He does not look the other way; He does not excuse. What does the sinless God do? He does the unimaginable. He imputes all our guilt, our blame, and our judgment to His beautiful, beloved, eternal Son. Jesus chose to endure in His own soul and body the just wrath of God for what we have done. He actually interposed His own sinless self between the righteous wrath of God and our sinfulness because He loves us with a deep, deep love. He hung naked, exposed, and unprotected under the retribution that the multitude of our iniquities deserves, but He has borne once and for all that guilt and condemnation. It was His unimaginable affection for these former rebels that kept Him there suspended by nails under the judgment of God on the cross until our debt had all been cleared to the last penny, and then He could cry out, "It is finished!" (John 19:30).

Do you realize what He was doing? He was not offering His sufferings only. He was not offering His blood only. He was not offering His obedience only. He was not offering His human nature only. He was offering Himself without spot to God. Because Jesus Christ went to the cross, there is now no retribution whatsoever for us. The Lord Jesus has exhausted the utter totality of everything that our sins merit. Christ's payment of our debt means that God can never again make another demand for condemnation. He has once and for all condemned these sins on the cross of His Son. He has no desire or need to condemn them again in all whose hopes are in the work Christ completed. Because of Golgotha the condemnation has been exhausted. It is now as if our sins never were. The guilt has all been removed. There is nothing left about which God can be angry. That is what our propitiating Savior has achieved all by Himself. A great satisfaction for everything has been rendered by God to God. What is left undone and unforgiven? God has overlooked nothing.

Imagine a wagon train crossing the vast American prairies, and one day they see smoke from a prairie fire behind them. That day the wind is blowing strongly in their direction, and the fire is catching up with them. They encourage their horses to go faster and faster, but the flames are catching up on them and there is no river nearby into which they can drive their wagons. The horses are exhausted; they can now smell the fire and hear the crackling flames. Then the wagon master halts all the wagons and he rides a hundred yards in front of them, and he does the unthinkable. He gets out his tinder box and sets fire to the prairie in front of them. Is he going crazy? Is this a horrible suicide? The flames are catching up on them, and now in front of them are the spreading flames of this man-made fire. They are in despair. But soon the wagon master gives another order: "Drive onto the burned-over ground!" So they do, and soon the great prairie fire catches up with them, but when it comes to the burned ground it can go no farther. The fire parts, goes around them, and leaves them hot and coughing but alive as they stand on that safe place.

The flames of God's wrath cannot burn up sinners for the same sin twice. If they have fallen on Christ and consumed Him as He was made sin for us, then they cannot also fall on us. Jesus is the Lamb of God who has taken away the sins of all who have gone to Him for refuge. There is therefore now no retribution left for those who are in Christ Jesus.

We who have entrusted ourselves to Him receive the blessing of divine appeasement and so we are completely safe.

We can run into the presence of a sin-hating God, and He will welcome us as His children, with smiles and smiles forever. He has put the door handle into His presence so low that the smallest, dirtiest, smelliest child who believes on Him can reach it, open the door, and come just as they are at any time to talk to their loving Father. He smiles at them in welcome, never too busy to hear what they have to say.

Are you satisfied with what the Lord Christ has done? Are you completely satisfied with what He has achieved? Let your conscience be satisfied with it. Let your intellect be satisfied with it. Let your past be satisfied with it. Let your worst mistake be satisfied with it. If God is satisfied with it, then you can be satisfied with it. Let the sins of the chief of sinners (and he might be reading this) be satisfied as he along with every Christian hides in the Lord Jesus Christ the Savior.

7

REDEMPTION

The cross was Christ purchasing our redemption.

This was the favored word of the Lord Jesus when He came to explain to the world the meaning of His own death: "The Son of Man did not come to be served, but to serve, and to give His life a ransom for many" (Matt. 20:28). Now, this word *ransom* refers to the cost of delivering someone from captivity. For instance, hostages are released if their families can raise enough money to pay the ransom price. Until then these prisoners are held captive. The twelve tribes of Israel had to be redeemed from their Egyptian captivity. You and I and everyone else need to be redeemed, as we see in this significant statement found in Galatians 3:22: "The Scriptures declare that we are all prisoners of sin" (NLT). Do you see the *authority* in that statement? The Scriptures declare it. Do you see the *universality* of that statement? The whole world is imprisoned—no exceptions, no, not one. Do you see the *divine evaluation* of the state of all mankind? All people are prisoners of sin. There are no exceptions; sin has got everybody in its power. It comes to every man and woman, every boy and girl; it has gained mastery over the whole human race.

The worldly wise who surround people who appear to have some interest in the faith say such things as, "You can't be believing in a *personal* God. You don't really believe that Jesus Christ is the *Son of God*, do you? Life terminates in death, and at that moment we are all extinguished—snuffed out like a candle flame. Seek your excitement wherever you can while you are breathing. Go for it! Do things your way. Enjoy your liberty. You are the captain of your fate. You are the master of your soul. Worship whatever suits you. Idolize your own choice in life. Never read the Bible. Never go to a gospel church. Never think of your own soul. Banish thoughts of death and eternity from your mind. Never pray; it is pointless. When someone gives you a leaflet about the message of Christianity, thank him with a smile, put it in your pocket, and later discard it. Never read it. When someone starts to talk to you about Jesus Christ, change the subject. Encourage your whole family to disregard the claims of the Lord Jesus Christ just as you do."

That is what the worldly wise remorselessly repeat to all they meet, day after day, persuading them that they alone really are the free ones. The reaction of all the gullible world is to nod in agreement, saying, "Yes, you are right. Let me go on enjoying my freedom from all of that *religion business*." But far from true freedom, mankind is experiencing an intellectual and spiritual life of abject slavery. Men's existence, day after day, year after year, is a life lived under the domination of sin. Of course, everyone has a kind of freedom. None of us are a puppet. We are like a convict in his cell who can freely decide on such activities as reading a book or watching TV or having a nap or choosing what pair of socks he is going to wear that day—a real free will for all the trifling things. But he is utterly incapable of getting out of his cell and leaving the prison. He cannot escape that!

Man's great need is emancipation from the authority of sin that dominates his life. He needs to be redeemed from its power over him. He should be longing for the day when he can cry, "Free at last! My chains are broken! The prison doors are open!" Charles Wesley was a man who experienced the liberation that Christ had won for him. He wrote these words that describe the beginning of the Christian pilgrimage:

> Long my imprisoned spirit lay
> Fast bound in sin and nature's night;
> Thine eye diffused a quick'ning ray,
> I woke, the dungeon flamed with light;
> My chains fell off, my heart was free;
> I rose, went forth, and followed Thee.[1]

Such is a typical Christian response, rejoicing in deliverance from the power of sin. But what is the cause of this deliverance? It is no sum of money that we have collected ourselves. We did not pay a single penny for our ransom. Jesus is the one. On Him alone we call. We had incurred an enormous debt that we could never pay, but Christ has paid it all. Such a costly deliverance was accomplished by the Lord Jesus Christ on Calvary. There He permitted Himself to become so vulnerable and accessible to the power of sin. He handed Himself over to the unrelenting menace of wickedness. I can imagine

---

1. Charles Wesley, "And Can It Be, That I Should Gain?," in the public domain.

Lucifer commanding all the demons in the pit to go forth and focus all their malice on Christ as He hung on the cross.

But our Lord took it all! He bore the intensity of their hellish, fiendish rage toward Him. Far from succeeding in spoiling Jesus's mission to redeem us, the prince of darkness and all his legions utterly failed to deflect Him from what He was doing in saving us on the cross. Our brave Savior faced them unflinchingly and "disarmed principalities and powers, He made a public spectacle of them, triumphing over them in it" (Col. 2:15). He took everything they had to offer and never turned aside or cried to be delivered. From that track He turned not back. And when He knew that He had paid the full redemption price, He cried aloud, "It is finished!" (John 19:30). There was not a single one He had been entrusted by His Father to redeem whom He failed to deliver, even the very worst of all sinners. Redemption to the last penny was paid in full; He overcame all the legion of demons that had come upon Him in the darkness of that day. He crushed Satan's head. He slew the great dragon. He overthrew the prince of darkness. He did not negotiate with the devil! He overcame him. The Lord Christ had already demonstrated this when He encountered the worst case of demon possession that the world has ever witnessed. I am referring to that legion of demons that possessed the two Gergesenes. These demons were ejected from the possessed men by a mere word of Jesus, all in the twinkling of an eye, and directed into the herd of swine (Matt. 8:28–34).

We must remember this, that those who are joined to Christ, and are in Him forevermore, were joined to Him in His death on the cross. They have triumphed over the bondage of sin and Satan, all through the might of the Lord. They now are made capable of saying no to unbelief, to temptations, and to betraying the gospel. They can do all things through Christ, who moment by moment strengthens them. They have been released from their forlorn captivity. Their ransom has been paid in full and they are redeemed.

However deeply you have fallen into sin, even dabbling in the occult and becoming involved in the most unspeakable activities, the Lord Christ is greater in power than all the forces of darkness working in united hatred against you. "Be released!" cries the Mighty One who spoiled those principalities and powers on Golgotha, leaving them vanquished, disorganized, and in wretched despair by His redeeming death and His resurrection on the third day. "Be released!" He has commanded. Once you are free, you become the light of the world. You are the salt of the earth through Him. That is what He has done for us. Hear these great words of the apostle to Titus: "[He] gave Himself for us, that He might redeem us from every lawless deed and purify for Himself His own special people, zealous for good works" (Titus 2:14). Mighty divine power alone can redeem sinners.

To whom was the redemption price paid? It was not at all due to Satan. To the devil we owe nothing but our scornful wrath. The price paid was at a retributive, substitutionary, propitiatory, and redeeming cost, and such a price could be paid only by the Son of God to His Father. Our sins have incurred an infinite debt, not because they are infinite in number or quality but because they are committed against an infinitely holy God. Man owes God, and only the immeasurable God can pay an immeasurable debt. But man's debt must be paid by man. Angels cannot pay it for us. Hence, God became man, and this God-man paid the price for our redemption. Jesus of Nazareth offered Himself without blemish to God. In salvation we open our hands and hearts to receive this gift from the Holy One; we get an accomplished redemption. What a gift! We have been redeemed, not with corruptible things such as silver or gold but with the precious blood of our Savior.

The curse of sin is the holy denunciation of God on everything that defiles and cheapens and dehumanizes mankind, but Christ has redeemed us from that curse, "having become a curse for us (for it is written, 'Cursed is everyone who hangs on a tree')" (Gal. 3:13). We live our lives day by day as those whose hopes are all exclusively in the saving work of our Lord; we exist now, minute by minute, day after day, year by year, under the constant kindness of a loving heavenly Father. Every spiritual blessing has replaced the cursed judgment of the law from which we are now released. Farewell, curse! Welcome, God's blessings in Christ!

Of course, all the unbelieving world has benefited to some degree from the dying love of Jesus Christ. All the ancillary benefits that God in His mercy bestows on a rebel world—like health and intelligence and prosperity and the blessings of family life and a peaceful nation—come via the cross, but redemption and forgiveness of sins and eternal life are bought only for all who have turned from their sin and believed. "Call His name Jesus, for He will save His people from their sins," said the messenger of God to Joseph, Mary's husband (Matt. 1:21). In other words, Jesus bought *some* blessings for all people, but He secured *all* blessings only

Today between all mankind and our Creator God there is alienation and bitterness. You see what happened in Eden, how our federal head Adam along with Eve proceeded to do what God forbade. They defied their loving Lord; they took the fruit from the tree that He had told them explicitly not to take. The immediate consequence was mankind's guilt and shame, and they went into hiding. Our first parents had been defiant and rebellious, and now they were in great need of a lasting reconciliation between themselves and God. But how did they respond? They didn't break their hearts and fall on the ground before God and weep out their guilt and shame. They chose rather to make excuses! Adam blamed Eve. The serpent was blamed. They had no words of affection for their kind and loving Lord. Eden had been a place where humans lived in harmony with their dear Lord, with each other, and with the environment. Then the situation changed irrevocably. They were driven out, and at the gate stood an angel with a flaming sword. Humanly speaking, the way of reconciliation was closed, blocked by the flaming holiness of an offended deity.

What happened to end the stalemate of cold inactivity? It is God who initiated and began to set up the machinery of reconciliation. He searched them out and talked to them, made coverings for them from animal skins, and announced what He would certainly do to the lying serpent: He would crush his head, and He would prepare the Seed of the woman to come and establish a divine reconciliation.

The Lord is the one who had been wronged, but this same Lord is the one who started to put things right. That is grace! That is the teaching of Christ in the Sermon on the Mount:

"First be reconciled to your brother" (Matt. 5:24). Who is being urged to be reconciled? It is not the one who harbors resentment and keeps us at arm's length but rather the one who is worshiping God and realizes in a moment that his brother has a festering resentment against him. "Go and be reconciled to him, and then you can offer your gift to God." In other words, you go as a beneficiary of grace henceforth to change your brother's bad attitude toward yourself. You deal with that. You speak to him, showing him patience and kindness, wanting reconciliation. So, too, the innocent God has come to us rebels and has dealt with the wrong that we have committed against Him. Now we must deal with whatever He has against us and make peace with the one we've provoked by all our sin.

The human way of reconciliation is very different. The innocent man in the dispute shrugs. "I am the wronged party and am waiting for him to apologize." The one who has done wrong, who has been provocative, who has caused the estrangement is the one who has to take the initiative. He must go and apologize. It is the guilty one who has to do everything in his power to humble himself and deal with the root cause of the alienation and seek to reconcile. He must eat humble pie; he has to acknowledge how foolish and wrong he has been. We do not like doing that. We often half-heartedly mumble, "Well, if I have done anything to offend you…" If? No! No ifs, we must be open and straight and bow before the one we have wronged and say, "I was bad; I was dreadful, and I am sorry. Please accept my regret." Until we do that we can do nothing about establishing acceptance, forgiveness, and reconciliation.

How utterly different is God's way. He is the blameless one. He is the one who has been wronged, and yet He is the one who deals with the root cause of the estrangement. After the fall there was disharmony between man and God. Man became defensive and self-excusing, feeling nothing; but the innocent God experienced the pain of man's rebellion, estranged actions, coldness of heart, and pride. Man entered such a horrible condition, ignoring God, shaking his fist at the God he had offended, determined to live without Him. What a picture of ugliness, like some festering carbuncle, stinking and bursting with puss.

What does God do? He takes all that huge evil lump, every atom of guilt, every molecule of sin, and He removes it all, everything that has caused the estrangement, and then He lays it all—all of it!—on His divine Son on the cross. He imputes the lot to the blameless Lord Christ. He makes the sinless one to be sin. He did not cause the alienation. We did that, but He becomes the one who deals with it. We defied God and pursued riotous living, yet it was the loving Lord who removed the blame forever, who paid the price of the reconciliation, who ended the estrangement. That is what the Lord Christ achieved for a multitude of people who now are bending in worship before Him.

That has all been achieved by His actions alone. The reconciliation is all God's work, His grand prerogative. God reconciles Himself to rebels by the sacrifice of the cross. Reconciliation was not some joint enterprise, fifty-fifty, so that we can coolly nod our heads and say, "Yep, it was the best thing I ever did to be reconciled to God." Jesus did not do 90 percent of the job on Calvary, leaving 10 percent to be done by us. He, all by Himself, removed 100 percent of all that we'd done wrong. God reconciled all thing to Himself by His Son. He has covered all our sin—all our past sin, all our present sin, all our future sin—forever, and in this way He has reconciled the holy and righteous God to us. He has received every bit of our guilt and removed it eternally from us. So my sins in the sight of God are as though they never were. They do not control or modify my relation to God. There is no defilement and no alienation at all. The sin-hating God has nothing to focus His wrath on. It has all been put on Christ and exhausted there, and so we are whiter than snow. God loves us as He loves His own Son, for He has joined us to Him; because we are in Him, there is therefore now no condemnation left for us. God, having loved us, has proceeded to reconcile us to Himself.

How do we know that? How can we be certain? I will tell you. Because of the resurrection of the Lord Jesus from the dead. Because the tomb was empty, His body was no longer there, and He appeared many times to different groups of men and women, hundreds of people, for forty days. That resurrected life was the vindication of Jesus, a declaration by His Father, and through the Holy Spirit, saying that our sin is all forgiven and there is no barrier whatsoever, no impediment. There is absolutely nothing left. The single determinant of your relationship with God today is what happened on that cross. Nothing else matters. Nothing else is relevant. There are only two factors in the equation: what Christ did and how God responded. Your ups and downs and failures are irrelevant. The one thing relevant for you regarding your relation with God and to eternal life is what Jesus Christ did on that cross. So now we can sing,

> My God is reconciled,
> His pard'ning voice I hear;
> He owns me for a child,
> I can no longer fear.
> With confidence I now draw nigh,
> With confidence I now draw nigh,
> And "Father, Abba, Father," cry.[1]

The ministry of the gospel church is to inform the world of the achievements of a reconciling God. The entire ministry of reconciliation consists of an explanation of what has transpired and a pleading with men and women to take advantage of this mighty work of God and to be reconciled to Him. The reconciliation between every believing, repentant disciple and the God who is light, in whom is no darkness at all, is complete. Reconciliation never can or will be repeated because there is no need of another reconciliation. It is over, finished, perfect. Jesus Christ accomplished everything He intended to do, and there is peace with God accomplished by His work, and His work alone is superabundant. He does not need to perform any other acts of reconciliation. Often our work is inadequate. We make mistakes, and so what we did needs to be done again, better, until we get it right. The Lord of Glory got it right the first time. He has no need to repeat any aspect of His achievements on Golgotha.

---

1. Charles Wesley, "Arise, My Soul, Arise," Hymnary.org, accessed August 10, 2023, https://hymnary.org/text/arise_my_soul_arise_shake_off_thy_guilty.

Has He brought all the people of God into a state of eternal security so that they can affirm, "More happy, but not more secure, the glorified spirits in heaven"?[2] The Scripture gives us a resounding "Yes!" There are no more offerings for sin needed. Golgotha is a resounding success.

---

2. Augustus M. Toplady, "A Debtor to Mercy Alone," in the public domain.

9

SATISFACTION

The cross was where Christ satisfied the living God.

Three hymns have become immensely popular all over the world in the last twenty years. The first is an old hymn written by an Irish minister's daughter named Charitie Lees Bancroft (nee Smith). It is "Before the Throne of God Above." One striking aspect is that its profound theology and deep personal devotion came from a young woman about twenty years old, today the typical age of a university student. This early hymn of hers was first published when she was twenty-two, and she lived for a further sixty years, dying in 1923. A fine modern tune has caused the rediscovery of the hymn. It contains these striking lines:

> Because the sinless Savior died,
> My sinful soul is counted free;
> For God the Just is satisfied
> To look on Him and pardon me.[1]

God is satisfied with everything that Christ has done.

---

1. Charitie Lees Bancroft, "Before the Throne of God Above," in the public domain.

The next contemporary hymn to refer to the satisfaction of God at the achievements of Christ is "He Will Hold Me Fast," originally by Ada Habershon. I would hear my mother singing this hymn around our home in the 1940s as she did her household chores, but a new tune has been written to it and a new verse added by Matt Merker so that this hymn has been resurrected and now is sung all over the world:

> Justice has been satisfied;
> He will hold me fast.

In this hymn there is a narrowing of the satisfaction: God Himself, in particular His justice, is being satisfied.

The same approach is found in a third contemporary hymn that refers to the fact of divine satisfaction. It is "In Christ Alone," the first hymn written by Stuart Townend and Keith Getty in 2001. It swiftly became immensely popular and spread everywhere, and it also contains a reference to our Lord's death on the cross as an action causing divine satisfaction:

> Till on that cross as Jesus died
> The wrath of God was satisfied.

Those particular lines made the hymn a focus of criticism by religious opponents of the conviction that the Bible teaches that the wrath of God was satisfied at the death of His Son. In 2013, a fifteen-member committee of the Presbyterian Church (USA) decided to exclude the hymn from a new church hymnal after Townend and Getty refused permission to alter the second line of the above stanza so that it could sung as "the love of God was magnified." The committee announced that it was not so much the word *wrath* that bothered them but the word *satisfied*. This sparked off a debate in the United States that spread across denominational lines. Is it right to say that God was satisfied by the death of His Son? Is the very concept of divine satisfaction alien to Christianity and to relationships between men and between man and God?

In post-apartheid South Africa, the Truth and Reconciliation Commission made satisfaction part of the process of enabling victims and oppressors to live together. Oppressors and victims had to face each other in a public place and listen to one another's stories. The satisfaction required was that the truth had to be declared, understood, and acknowledged by both parties. On a human level there has to be a place for satisfaction as part of the process of righting wrongs, publicly acknowledging accountability, making restitution if necessary, and healing memories to enable a deep and lasting reconciliation. It is about love being demonstrated corporately through justice being done and being seen to be done. So if God is satisfied at the work of His Son, we, too, must be satisfied. We are not people of resentment and bitterness, because God has become patient and forgiving to those who have done great harm to us or to those we love. They have repented and put their hopes in the work of Jesus Christ and they are ransomed and forgiven. If God says to them, "No condemnation," then that must be our attitude to them too. We are not to respond like Ananias and many in the early church who heard that Saul of Tarsus had become a Christian (Acts 9:13–14). They were dissatisfied with this development as if God was not in the know as to how wicked Saul had been. But God knew of all the depravity of Saul of Tarsus and what he had done to the early church. God knew that all that sin had been borne by the Son of God on the cross, and God was satisfied with the new apostle Paul.

Our sins spoil even our best endeavors, but God has wrought total satisfaction by what He Himself has done through His holy child. We Christians have to think of satisfaction in terms of the new covenant relationship between God and His people. Without the surety of divine satisfaction in the fractured relationship that exists between God and man, we become frozen in enmity. It is exclusively through Jesus Christ that God has become satisfied with our imperfect service and lives. There are good reasons for affirming the death of Christ as divinely satisfying.

First, unless the death of Christ were an absolute necessity, how could Golgotha be demonstrating divine love? Paul tells the Galatians that Christ had loved him and had given Himself for him (Gal. 2:20). The Lord Jesus Himself said, "Greater love has no one than this, than to lay down one's life for his friends" (John 15:13). Such love makes sense only if the friend should be in terrible danger. Golgotha makes no sense if it is inessential grandstanding! If Christ's death were not utterly necessary, how could it demonstrate the Father's love? Why sacrifice His Son if it could have been avoided? That would be pure horror! There must be some issue to be resolved between God and man that demanded nothing less than the crucifixion of the Son of God. John 3:16 is the classic gospel verse; it declares that to save the world from perishing, God gave His own Son—to Calvary. He spared Him not. There was no alternative, no lesser cup available for the Lord to drink.

Second, unless the death of Christ were the only possible remedy for the human predicament, it could never serve as a demonstration of the righteousness of God. If exhortation to do one's best and a display of greater endeavor to righteous living were sufficient, then why would we have needed the cross of Jesus? Paul makes it transparently clear that God put forward Christ as a sacrifice to remit the sins of Old Testament believers who had shed the blood of pigeons, lambs, goats, and heifers, though quite aware that such deaths alone had to be utterly incapable of cleansing the souls of the people making sacrifice who had sinned. How could the death of an animal expiate the guilt of a man who had murdered another person? All those animal sacrifices were anticipatory types that were pointing forward to the anti-type of the death of the Lamb of God. Calvary continues to be the justification of everyone whose faith and hope ever since that mighty day have been in the person and the achievements of their Lord and their Savior, Jesus Christ (Rom. 3:25). In what way could His sacrifice be the ultimate proof that God is a just God? Only if it served some great goal that could not be achieved in any other way. His sacrifice served this end—the satisfaction of God, so that the Creator could remain just but also forgive the sins of the world. Father, Son, and Holy Spirit acted in unity for the protection and vindication of all His people.

The wrath of a sin-hating God surely requires that there be just retribution for the unrepentant oppressor. The Lord who loves righteousness inevitably hates injustice. How can the guilt of such transgressions be remitted? Only by God condemning sin in the body of His Son (Rom. 8:3). And what of you and me and our trespasses? "Do you think...that you will escape the judgment of God?" asks Paul (Rom. 2:3).

"Only through the mediation of His Son alone," the believer replies. There is just one place where divine satisfaction could be achieved—Golgotha!

Third, the death of Christ was necessary because sin deserves its condemnation. If we judge our sinful behavior to be a little collection of mere peccadillos, a few sexual indiscretions, some white lies, a little occasional overindulgence, then we will tend to reject the necessity of the Lord of heaven dying the death of the cross by the will of His Father to obtain mercy for morally limping men and women. We will think the prayer, "Forgive our foolish ways" sufficient. But if a sin is vastly more abhorrent—as obscene as David's was when he seduced the wife of a blameless and honorable man, impregnated her, and then murdered her good husband—we find that behavior intolerable and distressing. How hard to describe such actions as a man's foolish ways, but many other even more despicable cruelties than King David's occur every hour of the day. And if we cry out for justice for these, for a fair retribution of the unmentionable horrors from devilish men, then how much more should the living God care? Isn't every crime against a human being a crime against the image of God? Every sin is a defiance of God's majesty.

One enormous problem today is that sin is not explained to many congregations as they gather on a Sunday. Joanne Shetler worked among the Balangao people of the Philippines for many years translating the Bible into their language. Even before the New Testament was completed, the gospel was being proclaimed, and some of the people were becoming Christians. At their church meetings, finished portions of the New Testament translation were read aloud, "sometimes with surprising results," Shetler noted. She illustrated further:

There was on one particular Sunday a woman attending a service for the first time. She enjoyed the singing, but as they read the Scriptures, she became increasingly agitated. Finally, teeth clenched, she got up and walked out. Later, while they were eating, she stomped into the house of the missionaries Tony and Tekla, walking up to within inches of Tony and, in a fashion quite untypical of Balangaos, she accused him to his face. "The nerve of you! You invite me to your meeting and what do you do? You tell that man up in front of every sin I've committed, and he goes and announces it in public. And not only that, but he reads it from a book! I'll never come again."[2]

How rarely does such a blessed reaction occur, when the Spirit of God is present in our meetings and He convicts of sin and righteousness and judgment to come. The main reason that people today are unaware of their sin is that sin is not expounded from our pulpits. But in the Philippines, in their first years of hearing the Christian gospel, the Balangaos were convicted by Scripture's diagnosis of the human condition. Often the elders found it judicious to announce before reading from the Word that the people would likely think the elders knew something about them and were exposing it. They would have to explain that no one told them any secrets; rather, the Word itself uncovers hidden things. It's just the nature of the Bible. People were convicted of sin from the Word, and they came to understand that they needed a Savior from their sin.

---

2. Joanne Shelter and Patricia Purvis, *And the Word Came with Power: How God Met and Changed a People Forever* (Portland, Ore.: Multnomah, 1992), 104.

In the Western world sin is so endemic and taken for granted. All manner of behavior is shrugged off and excused. It is when people are convicted of the existence of a holy God and a coming day of judgment that the sin-bearing work of Christ becomes understandable and good news. We believe that Scripture declares that the cross satisfied a God estranged from us by our sinfulness. Consider this wondrous news, that through the divine satisfaction of the cross of Jesus Christ the enmity of a sin-hating God toward us no longer exists! So we, too, are satisfied with Jesus Christ because through Him God has become satisfied with us.

> Well of water, ever springing,
> Bread of life so rich and free,
> Untold wealth that never faileth,
> My Redeemer is to me.
> Hallelujah! I have found Him
> Whom my soul so long has craved!
> Jesus satisfies my longings,
> Thro' His blood I now am saved.[3]

Where is divine satisfaction taught in the Word of God? Consider the work of creation. On the first day, light was created, and God's response was satisfaction. He saw that it was good. The second day God created the sky and the sea, and He saw that that also was good. On the third day dry land, plants, and trees were created, and again God was satisfied with all He saw in oceans, prairies, and forests. The fourth day witnessed the creation of sun, moon, and stars, again, all

---

3. Clara T. Williams, "Satisfied," Hymnary.org, accessed August 10, 2023, https://hymnary.org/hymn/BH1991/539.

SATISFACTION

to the good pleasure of God. On the fifth day God created the birds and sea creatures, and that, too, satisfied the Lord. Finally, on day six, the land animals and man were made. "Then God saw everything that He had made, and indeed it was very good" (Gen. 1:31), and so the first chapter of the Bible ends with the satisfaction of God with His creation.

When we come to the work of redemption, we find the same pattern. The Old Testament sacrifices that the Lord instituted, when faithfully observed by worshipers, were described as "a sweet aroma to the LORD" (Lev. 1:13). Those Old Testament types find their fulfillment in the Lamb of God, who now takes away the sin not only of believing Jews but of the world. So the fulfillment of the Old Testament sacrifices as they pointed forward to the death of Christ are also described as a "sacrifice to God for a sweet-smelling aroma" (Eph. 5:2). In the book of Micah the prophet asks and answers the question, "With what shall I come before the LORD, and bow myself before the High God?" The prophet continues, "He has shown you, O man, what is good; and what does the LORD require of you but to do justly, to love mercy, and to walk humbly with your God?" (6:6, 8). "But who lives like that?" you ask. The answer, of course, is manifest in how the Son of God lived and died. He is the one who stood before His Father and bowed down before Him. He lived with total integrity the life of one who walked humbly with His Father. God, totally satisfied with His Son, exclaimed, "This is My beloved Son, in whom I am well pleased" (Matt. 3:17).

But there is in Scripture that warning, the contrast of certain sacrificial acts that plainly do not satisfy God at all, that even provoke Him to wrath, as we see in the opening chapter of Isaiah: "'To what purpose is the multitude of your sacrifices to Me?' says the LORD. 'I have had enough of burnt offerings of rams and the fat of fed cattle. I do not delight in the blood of bulls, or of lambs or goats'" (1:11). Religion alone does not save. Christ must save and Christ alone.

Again, in the vital portrait of the Suffering Servant of God in Isaiah 53, reference is made to the satisfaction of God. We read, "He shall see the labor of His soul, and be satisfied. By His knowledge My righteous Servant shall justify many, for He shall bear their iniquities" (v. 11). This passage is suggesting that one aspect of the sacrifice of the Servant is that it gives total satisfaction to His own mind and conscience. "I am satisfied with what I have offered to My Father." But that could be possible only if our Lord knew with certainty that His death on the cross had first of all given satisfaction to His Father, that it was acceptable to Him, that it was even a fragrant offering and "very good" in the evaluation of almighty God. The death of Jesus was in fact everything that God could possibly have desired. That is why the Lord Jesus had come into the world, and He was completely aware of that, and so He and the Holy Spirit were as satisfied as the Father. The inevitable question which that fact raises is whether we ourselves are satisfied with the work of Christ. Are our consciences satisfied? Is our past satisfied? Is our mind satisfied? If God is satisfied, then we must be. Always keep returning to the achievements of the dying love of Jesus Christ. Our hope is built on nothing less than that.

In one of the "Revival Year" sermons, preached on the morning of May 29, 1859, from a pulpit set up on the stage of the Music Hall of the Royal Surrey Gardens in London, twenty-four-year-old Charles Haddon Spurgeon was preaching on the glorious person who hung on the cross. In the course of the sermon he said,

> Note first the dignity of the victim who offered himself up to divine justice. Man had sinned; the law required the punishment of manhood. But Jesus, the eternal Son of God, "very God of very God," who had been hymned through eternal ages by joyous angels, who had been the favourite of his Father's court, exalted high above principalities and powers, and every name that is named, he himself condescended to become man; was born of the Virgin Mary; was cradled in a manger; lived a life of suffering, and at last died a death of agony. If you will but think of the wondrous person whom Jesus was—as very God of very God, king of angels, creator, preserver, Lord of all—I think you will see that in his sufferings, the law received a greater vindication than it could have done even in the sufferings of all the men that have ever lived or ever could live. If God had consumed the whole human race, if all the worlds that float in ether had been sacrificed as one mighty holocaust to the vengeance of the law, it would not have been so well vindicated as when Jesus died. For the deaths of all men and all angels would have been but the deaths and sufferings of creatures; but when Jesus died, the Creator himself underwent the pang, it was the divine preserver of the world hanging on the cross. There is such dignity in the Godhead, that all it does is marvellous and infinite in its merit; and when he stooped to suffer, when he bowed his awful head, cast aside his diadem of stars to have his brow girt about with thorns; when his hands that once swayed the sceptre of all worlds were nailed to

the tree; when his feet that erst had pressed the clouds, when these were fastened to the wood, then did the law receive an honour such as it never could have received if a whole universe in one devouring conflagration had blazed and burned for ever.[4]

So what is God satisfied with in the death of Christ? Consider the claims that our Creator makes on all men and women whom He has made in His own image and likeness, whom He blesses richly day by day. He is good to all His creatures who live and move and have their being in Him. But with these blessings there is an accompanying responsibility to God the great giver. Our father Adam had failed to give obedience to God, while Jesus Christ loved God with all His heart, soul, mind, and strength. Every claim God makes of the line of Adam was ultimately satisfied by the life and death of God's Son. He fulfilled all the demands of God's law by His righteous perfection; He satisfied God's just judgment of sin by the sacrifice of Himself. He accomplished this as the God-man. As God, His sacrifice was of infinite and eternal value. As man, He became our substitute and bore our condemnation. For all who repent and trust in Him, Christ has canceled the debt they owe to God and has bought for them mercy, righteousness, and eternal life. Mankind owed God the debt of obedience, but we have failed to clear that debt because we love darkness and do things our own way. We have no way at all of repaying the immense debt that we have accumulated day after day, night after night. And it is impossible for the

---

4. Charles Spurgeon, "Justice Satisfied," The Spurgeon Center, accessed August 10, 2023, https://www.spurgeon.org/resource-library/sermons/justice-satisfied/#flipbook/.

just God to simply cancel it and to look away, forgetting about it. That would be to put sin above and beyond God's law. The debt must be paid. It can only be paid by a sacrifice of even greater value than the original debt itself.

Anselm, the archbishop of Canterbury from 1093 to 1109, wrote an important book on this subject titled *Why God Became Man*, in which he affirmed that in accomplishing our salvation, "It is not enough merely to return what was taken away; in view of the insult committed, he must give back more than he took away."[5] Consider how man's sin has insulted an infinitely honorable God, how only a payment of infinite value would do.[6] That is precisely why God became man. No one *can* make satisfaction or pay the recompense except God, and no one *ought* to offer satisfaction except man. Anselm summarizes his conclusions like this:

> Now we must inquire how there can be a God-Man.... For God will not do it, because he does not owe it, and man will not do it, because he cannot. Therefore, for the God-Man to do this, the person who is to make this satisfaction must be both perfect God and perfect man, because none but the true God can make it, and none but true man owes it. Thus, while it is necessary to find a God-Man in whom the integrity of both natures is preserved, it is no less necessary for these two complete natures to meet in one person—just as body and

---

5. Anselm, *Why God Became Man*, ed. and trans. Eugene R. Fairweather, in *A Scholastic Miscellany: Anselm to Ockham*, The Library of Christian Classics: Icthus Edition (Philadelphia: Westminster Press, 1961), 1.11.

6. I have benefited from the helpful reflections of Donald Macleod, *Christ Crucified: Understanding the Atonement* (Downers Grove, Ill.: IVP Academic, 2014), 174.

rational soul meet in one man—for otherwise the same person could not be perfect God and perfect man.[7]

Anselm writes his book in the form of a dialogue with a novice named Boso, who lamely suggests that he could pay God for his sin with "repentance, a contrite and humble heart, fastings and all sorts of bodily labors, mercy in giving and forgiving, and obedience."[8] Anselm replies famously, "You have not yet considered what a heavy weight sin is."[9] As Augustus Toplady wrote so unforgettably,

> Not the labors of my hands
> Can fulfil thy law's demands;
> Could my zeal no respite know,
> Could my tears forever flow,
> All for sin could not atone;
> Thou must save, and thou alone.
>
> Nothing in my hand I bring,
> Simply to the cross I cling;
> Naked, come to thee for dress;
> Helpless, look to thee for grace;
> Foul, I to the fountain fly;
> Wash me, Savior, or I die.[10]

Imagine sincere grief lasting one year—365 days of nonstop tears, let alone tears *forever* flowing—and yet all that cannot achieve the total satisfaction of the just and holy One as we sin against Him. Only the God-man has achieved the

---

7. Anselm, *Why God Became Man*, 2.7.
8. Anselm, *Why God Became Man*, 1.20.
9. Anselm, *Why God Became Man*, 1.21.
10. Augustus Toplady, "Rock of Ages," in the public domain.

total satisfaction of God. Here is where we find a little inadequacy in the words of the new hymns when they say that the cross satisfied the wrath or the justice of God. That is certainly true, but Golgotha satisfied more than those awesome attributes. The work of the Son of God on the cross satisfied divine justice, divine love, divine grace, divine long-suffering. In other words, it satisfied God in all His attributes. It satisfied Father, Son, and Holy Spirit. All heaven is satisfied with what the Lord Christ has done. The cross is the supreme expression of divine mercy. God's forgiveness is grounded on His satisfaction, and without that satisfaction the accusing voice of sin and guilt would not have been silenced. Anselm wrote that sin which is neither paid for nor punished is the behavior of mere men and women who refuse to be subject to the law. Yet all creatures who live and move and have their being in God are accountable to His will; we all have to answer to our God. If God had demanded satisfaction from me personally and individually for all my wrongdoing, then that would have rendered my redemption impossible. There would be no hope for me at all if I had to present anything other than the Savior, the Son of God, as my hope of glory.

Hear again young Spurgeon's preaching in the Music Hall at Royal Surrey Gardens:

> If God had condemned each of us one by one, or the whole race in a mass, there would certainly have been a vindication of his justice. But lo! his own son takes upon him the sins of the world, and he comes before his Father's presence. He is not guilty in himself, but the sins of man are laid upon his shoulders. The Father condemns his Son; he gives him up to the Roman rod; he gives him up to Jewish mockery, to military scorn,

and to priestly arrogance. He delivers up his Son to the executioner, and bids him nail him to the tree; and as if that were not enough, since the creature had not power of itself to give forth all the vengeance of God upon its own substitute, God himself smites his Son. Are you staggered at such an expression? It is scriptural. Read in the fifty-third chapter of Isaiah, and there you have the proof thereof: "It pleased *the Lord* to bruise him: *he* hath put him to grief." When the whip had gone round to every hand, when the betrayer had smitten him, when Pilate and Herod, and Jew and Gentile, had each laid on the stroke, it was seen that human arm was not powerful enough to execute the full vengeance: then did the Father take his sword, and cry, "Awake! O sword, against my shepherd, against the man that is my fellow," and he smote him sternly, as if he had been his enemy, as if he were a common culprit, as if he were the worst of criminals—he smote him again and again, till that awful shriek was forced from the lips of the dying substitute,...my God, my God, why hast thou forsaken me? Surely, when God smites his Son, and such a Son, when God smites his only begotten and well-beloved, then Justice has more than its due, more than itself could ask, Christ himself did freely give![11]

So it was God Himself who provided the satisfaction. He became our satisfaction and bore the cost of our sins.

How was this satisfaction for our own sinning accomplished? By our union with the Lord Jesus Christ. Paul declares, "I have been crucified with Christ;...Christ lives in me" (Gal. 2:20). This is how the pain He bore and the

---

11. Spurgeon, "Justice Satisfied."

sufferings and forsakenness He endured all became connected to Paul and to me and to every single person joined by saving trust to the Lamb of God. Union with Christ, believing into Him, is the way the new covenant connects grace and status. Christ is married to His people, taking the responsibility for their debt and guilt and judgment as He joins them to Himself. That union is the perfect and secure position for everyone who has become one with Him by personally trusting in Him alone. Christ's passion is sufficient and superabundant because a complete, eternal, divine satisfaction has been made by Him, all by Himself, and all our vast debt to the Righteous One has been abolished. It is all gone. It no longer exists. If God is satisfied with what His Son has done, then can't I be also? Mustn't my conscience, my greatest guilt, my past all be satisfied with Jesus Christ? Guilty though I am and vile, can I not plead that this bloody sacrifice is enough to satisfy God's demands against me? Oh, yes, I know I am able to trust in Him!

If Christ once and for all offered Himself as the satisfaction of God's wrath against sinners, then *any sinner who comes to Him will find mercy.* Any sinner, and why not you?

> O perfect redemption, the purchase of blood,
> To every believer the promise of God;
> The vilest offender who truly believes,
> That moment from Jesus a pardon receives.[12]

William Cowper was an eighteenth-century English poet who suffered greatly from depression. His mother died when he was only six, and Cowper was sent to a boarding school

---

12. Fanny J. Crosby, "To God Be the Glory," in the public domain.

where the older boys mercilessly bullied and beat him. In his late twenties, he tried to commit suicide and was finally admitted to an insane asylum. William struggled with his guilt and would cry out for a fountain where he could find cleansing from his sin. The main doctor in the asylum was a committed Christian. He gently guided Cowper to the cross of Jesus Christ and the satisfaction our Lord provides. One day Cowper opened his Bible and saw, as if for the first time, these words in Romans 3:24–25: "Being justified freely by His grace through the redemption that is in Christ Jesus, whom God has set forth as a propitiation by His blood, through faith, to demonstrate His righteousness." Cowper responded, "Immediately I received strength to believe, and the full beams of the Sun of Righteousness shone on me. I saw the sufficiency of the atonement he had made, my pardon in his blood, and the fullness and completeness of his justification. In a moment I believed and received the gospel."[13] Cowper struggled with severe depression for the rest of his life, but God used him to write many beloved hymns. Cowper's experience—knowing that his sins were forgiven the instant that he believed in the shed blood of Jesus—could also be your experience. Trust in Jesus Christ now, because God is satisfied with what His beloved Son has done. He declares all who cast themselves on Christ "Not guilty!" both now and forever.

---

13. William Cowper, *Narrative of the Life of William Cowper, Esq.* (Birmingham: Beilby and Knotts, 1817), 60.

10

DESTRUCTION

It is in the death of Christ that death itself is mortified.

Professor John Murray returned to Badbea, Bonar Bridge, Sutherland (the home in which he was born) upon retiring from his long preaching career at Westminster Theological Seminary in Philadelphia. He spent the remaining years of his life, alas quite few, there with his new wife and two young children. He was often preaching in nearby churches. I had been in my charge in Aberystwyth for more than five years, and I invited him, my now elderly, former teacher, to come on the long journey south to preach for me in Wales on the Lord's Day. There is a special bond between a teacher and his students, and he could not refuse. Mr. Murray (as we always referred to him) preached a special message on the Friday evening of his first weekend in Wales, saying that "Christ was dead for our sins." Not that He died for them, which of course is true, but that He was dead for our sins. Let us consider what the Lord Jesus did for death by His own death on Golgotha.

What Is Death?

Death Is Penal

The death of men and women made in the image of God is unnatural and is a penalty for sinning. God warned Adam and Eve, "Of the tree of the knowledge of good and evil you shall not eat, for in the day that you eat of it you shall surely die" (Gen. 2:17). God carried out this judgment as soon as our first parents defied Him. The Lord cursed Adam with a life of heavy labor and his ultimate death: "In the sweat of your face you shall eat bread till you return to the ground, for out of it you were taken; for dust you are, and to dust you shall return" (Gen. 3:19). In 1 Corinthians 15 Paul highlights Adam's status as the federal head of humanity and his fall as the cause of physical death coming upon the whole human race. This is the historic biblical Christian view, that the sin of our father Adam and our own sin have exposed us to death.

Death Is the Rending Apart of Body and Soul

Men and women are what Christians call *psychosomatic unities*. Each man and woman is both body and soul. At death this union is destroyed. Upon his death, the spirit of the criminal who asked Jesus to remember him went immediately to paradise, where the Savior was waiting for him (Luke 23:43). When he had breathed his last breath, he was taken down from the cross and thrown into a pit to decay. He had been made from dust, and to dust he (that is, his body) was returned.

Death Is a Curse

The curse I am speaking of is separation from God. It was not "Man henceforth is to be cut off from God forever," eternally estranged from Him and under His judgment. Rather, God placed on us all the curse of physical death, and so He was providing the way to redeem believing, repenting men and women back to Himself. In the person of Jesus Christ, He himself suffered that curse of forsakenness from God.

Death Is a Regular Wage

This wage is earned when men continue to obey the sin that has mastered them. Our first parents immediately began to suffer as they experienced pain, estrangement, and the sensation of dying. This occurred in many ways, and who can tell what went on in the souls of our first parents when the consequences of defying their Lord fell upon them? Their wage for disobeying God was immediate; their closeness with God vanished instantly—no more walking with their Lord in the cool of the day. Their communion with each other was spoiled, they lost the Edenic garden, they saw one son kill another son, and much more. It was a rotten wage that they'd earned; they'd gotten a bad deal from the serpent.

Death Is an Enemy

How speedily our life shoots by. We reach our fifties, and one day this thought hits us that most of our lifespan is over and that so little has been achieved. We attend the funeral of younger relatives, see the grief, and hear the sobs. Death is tough enough to consider when it is the coffin of an old disciple being lowered into the grave, but to see that casket containing someone who firmly kept the Lord Jesus out of his life, or to know this teenager had hardly begun her pilgrimage, in such cases it hits us that death is a foreign intruder perverting normalcy; it is our intrepid and final enemy.

Death Is an Agony

In his Pentecost speech to his fellow Israelites, Peter talks straight to the thousands of men listening to him about the "pains [or agony] of death" (Acts 2:24). Death is decay. It is a place to which we commit ourselves and are abandoned eternally. There is a realm of the dead. Death is like a sentient being, an evil wrestler pinning down the dead, something that resolutely keeps its hold on them, never letting them go.

> In our culture it's taboo to speak of the agony of death. Instead, we much prefer resting in peace.... Yet no-one speaks more about the agony of death than Jesus. Jesus spent much of his ministry in Jerusalem pointing to the local rubbish tip—where the fires kept burning the trash of the town—saying "this is what the agony of death is like." He said death is a place where the worm doesn't stop eating—where the fire is not quenched (Mark 9:48). Jesus talks the most about the agonising reality of this unliving yet ongoing realm of the dead. Not resting in peace. Not "no more suffering." Not the injustice of the same simple annihilation of Hitler as for the nice old lady across the street, who always said hello while she gardened away the Springtime in the front yard.[1]

No, says Jesus. The agony of death is an eternally conscious state of decay, where we endure the agony that comes from our defiant contempt of the living God. There He removes all traces of His lovely image and withdraws from sinners any of the goodness and beauty they may have

---

1. Dave Bailey, "The Agony of Death," Living Church, accessed August 10, 2023, https://livingchurch.org.au/the-agony-of-death-2/.

received and experienced in their life on earth. There is the absence of loving relationships. There is the awareness of receiving what is justly deserved. It's no longer being able to hide behind claims of an innocent agnosticism. It's recognizing that they had determined to do things their own way, not His. The agony of physical, emotional, spiritual pain is the culminating sentence of a lifetime of rejecting God. It's the agony of receiving from God exactly what they had always asked for from Him—being left alone to live an existence without His intrusions of fatherly love.

Death Is Doubly Threatening
Death is drawing increasingly nearer every passing day. It is lying at the door, waiting, hiding, ready to pounce. What a threat! After our personal physical death there is a personal "second death." You have not heard of it? Has the world kept from you the reality of the second death? Or is there a refusal on your part to entertain the thought of eternal separation from God?

Whatever our initial reactions, this reference to a second death underlines just how much the wrath of God is revealed against sins of every kind: "The cowardly, unbelieving, abominable, murderers, sexually immoral, sorcerers, idolaters, and all liars shall have their part in the lake which burns with fire and brimstone, which is the second death" (Rev. 21:8). Three other places in the last book of the New Testament also mention the second death. One contains a hope of deliverance, which comes from hearing what the Holy Spirit is saying to us: "He who has an ear, let him hear what the Spirit says to the churches. He who overcomes shall not be hurt by the second death" (Rev. 2:11). When the Spirit is bearing witness to your spirit concerning the fact that Jesus is the Son of God, do you refuse to hear? Do you grieve the Spirit? Or do you overcome your hostility by listening to the Spirit speaking to you?

Again we are told, "Blessed and holy is he who has part in the first resurrection. Over such the second death has no power, but they shall be priests of God and of Christ, and shall reign with Him a thousand years" (Rev. 20:6). None who have been raised to share in the glories of the new heavens and new earth have any fear of the second death. They are blessed and holy people whose future is to serve God as priests and corulers with Christ.

Finally, those who should fear the second death are also described in the scenes of triumph that characterize the victory of the Lamb of God: "Then Death and Hades were cast into the lake of fire. This is the second death. And anyone not found written in the Book of Life was cast into the lake of fire" (Rev. 20:14–15). The huge hope for eternity is that a time is coming when death and the grave will be cast into the cosmic incinerator. But not one person whose names are recorded in the Book of Life will face that ultimate judgment. In other words, those who are born twice (once physically and once spiritually) will suffer just one death, while those who are born but once (physically) suffer two deaths.

Can you find any major difference between the description of the second death in the book of Revelation and the words of Jesus in the Sermon on the Mount? In Matthew 5:22, Jesus severely warns His listeners against anger and insult toward a brother or sister in the faith, alerting them to the fact that this will make them "in danger of the judgment." Then Jesus speaks of adultery and explains that it is not just a matter of physical action; it is more fundamentally a matter of the heart. For a man to look at a woman with lust is to have "committed adultery with her in his heart" (v. 28). Furthermore, breaking the seventh commandment, even in our hearts, makes us deserving of hell. So severe is that fate that it would be better for us to tear out an eye and throw it away if it is causing us to lust, because "it is more profitable for you that one of your members perish, than for your whole body to be cast into hell" (v. 29). The Lord Christ warned of the second death.

Elsewhere He is quoted as describing the danger to which sin leads as being "cast into hell fire" (Matt. 18:9). Again, Jesus warns not only that God's final judgment of unforgiven sin will be the "hell fire" but that it will be the "fire that shall never be quenched" (Mark 9:43). This statement is expanded thus: "It is better for you to enter the kingdom of God with one eye, rather than having two eyes, to be cast into hell fire—where 'Their worm does not die and the fire is not quenched'" (vv. 47–48). The first spokesman for the second death was our Lord Jesus Himself.

How the Lamb of God Dealt with Death by His Death
He Destroyed Death's Power over Us
The Son of God added to His divine person flesh and blood, born of a virgin, made in every point as we are, sin excepted, "that through death He might destroy him who had the power of death, that is, the devil" (Heb. 2:14). On the cross Christ was assaulted by all the powers from the pit surrounding Him, seeking to destroy Him by turning Him from His mission and thus tempting Him to sin. They utterly failed.

He spoiled all their devices and died triumphing over them. He crushed the head of Satan. He propitiated the wrath of a sin-hating God. The devil, then, has no power over any of us who are in Christ. He seeks to make us afraid of death, but we have been translated from the kingdom of Satan and are now in Christ forever. We are not in the guilt of our many sins—not in a single sin. We are in Christ. So we must live by that trust in our Savior's triumph and have no fear of death, Satan, or hell. We fill our minds with the triumph of the captain of our salvation.

He Has Freed Us from the Dominion and Despair of Death
We are not delivered from Satan's fiery darts of doubt and worry, but we have been delivered from believing the lying despair of the devil.

There was once a small boy who was afraid of going to the thicket at the bottom of their large garden. A malicious person had filled him with fear by telling stories of ogres and wicked fairies who lived there. His older brother knew this, and so one day he took this small boy to the edge of the trees and said, "I will go on and show you that there is absolutely nothing to fear there." His little brother cried and pleaded with him not to go: "Don't go! Please don't go! Stay here!" "It will be perfectly all right," his brother told him, and off he walked into the bushes and trees. Soon all the younger brother could hear was older sibling singing as he walked about:

> I'd rather have Jesus than silver or gold;
> I'd rather be His than have riches untold;
> I'd rather have Jesus than houses or lands.
> I'd rather be led by His nail pierced hand.

> Than to be the king of a vast domain
> Or be held in sin's dread sway.
> I'd rather have Jesus than anything
> This world affords today.[2]

After five minutes he returned smiling to his brother. "There is nothing to be afraid of there—nothing whatsoever! Come with me! Hold my hand and see." From that moment on the one abiding memory this boy had of that former place of fear was his darling brother, going there alone, singing and returning with a bright smile on his face. Then, joined to him, the fearful boy went hand in hand along the same safe path.

Someday soon God will send for each one of us to take us to our new home. There is no fear in that summons or in the new journey into such uncharted territory. When we have to go we will be confronted and surrounded by love as we have never known it, for heaven is a world of love. We will be welcomed by Someone who has always loved us, who has prayed day by day for us, who has been waiting for our arrival. He has prepared a lovely place for us.

He Has Made Death Impotent to Separate Us from the Love of God

The conquering captain of our salvation says to us that nothing whatsoever in this world or in heaven or hell is capable of separating us from the love of God. At the very beginning of His ministry He overcame the temptation of the devil in the wilderness. Even at His weakest, when nailed to a cross and assaulted by Satan, nothing could weaken his loving grip on

---

2. Rhea F. Miller, "I'd Rather Have Jesus," in the public domain.

all He was dying to save. The powers of hell could not take the weakest lamb from the flock of our good shepherd. Not even death could do it, for He rose the third day in the power of an endless life, and all His trusting people rose in Him. He ascended to the right hand of the majesty on high, and we are seated there in the heavenlies in Him. God loves us with a love that will never let us go, not even the Christian novice. It is the tenderest love with the most irresistible force, and this affection is "in Christ Jesus our Lord" (Rom. 8:39). It is the very same love with which God the Father loves His only begotten Son. We are partakers of a divine affection. He chose us in Christ, saved us in Christ, has kept us in Christ, and nothing is capable of separating us from His love. He chose us and blessed us as those He has united to Himself. He has made Jesus our Lord, Head, Husband, and Redeemer. We are safe!

> Should all the hosts of death
> And pow'rs of hell unknown
> Put their most dreadful forms
> Of rage and mischief on,
> I shall be safe, for Christ displays
> Superior pow'r and guardian grace.[3]

He Has Taken Away the Bitter Taste of Death
We are told that the Lord Jesus actually tasted death (Heb. 2:9). This metaphor is not intended to soften the phrase "he died" but rather strengthens it. He did not take a sip of death. He drained the cup of death in all its dread bitterness. He, the Holy One who had never sinned, tasted all that was in death. A man may die instantaneously by a guillotine or a bullet to

---

3. Isaac Watts, "Jesus, My Great High Priest," in the public domain.

the brain, but Christ hung on the cross for hours, and though they sought to dull His pain by giving Him wine and myrrh to drink, He refused it. He emptied the cup of death, swallow after swallow. He knew more than anyone what death was like before dying. He tasted it so that we never shall. For every believer, for the most doubting Christian, Christ has tasted and consumed death itself so that you will never experience its bitterness and dread. He knows what you fear far better than you and I know it. Do not be afraid.

He Has Removed the Sting of Death
Sin is death's dangerous weapon. Death gets you by stabbing you with sin. Once you sin, you die. Death is the consequence of sin because sin is the instrument—the stinger—by which death convicts and condemns human beings.

Consider a bee sting. When it stings you its stinger can't be removed by the bee. It is there, buried into your skin, and the bee's attempts to remove it are fatal for the insect. It only succeeds in pulling out its own entrails, and the bee dies. The sting of sin pierced deeply into Christ, and there was no way that Satan could extract that stinger to strike you. It has been received and dealt with comprehensively by Christ. Death is doomed; the sting of sin has been imputed to the body and soul of Christ on the cross and secured to Him far stronger than the nails that held Him to the cross. They were removed later that day; eternity will never remove our condemnation from the spotless Lamb. Death now holds no threat for all whose sin has been received by the Lord Christ. Its sting can't hurt you; its lethal venom cannot affect you; sin cannot take you into the lake of fire.

With the problem of sin gone, death has lost its power. Without its stinger, death can no longer claim human lives. This is why the resurrection is so important: resurrection from the dead, among other things, means that sin is now harmless in all its boasting and threatening. Sin is merely showboating. It has been conquered. By removing death's stinger, Christ has conquered death. Without sin, death is nothing but a harmless butterfly. It is taunted by the apostle Paul in 1 Corinthians 15:54–55: "Death is swallowed up in victory. O Death, where is your sting? O Hades, where is your victory?"

He Was Dead for Our Sins, but Only for Three Days

Death stood in the ring with Christ and sought to kill Him, but at a predetermined time the bell rang and the one-sided but brutal fight was all over. Our Lord Jesus rose triumphant over death.

> Death cannot keep its prey, Jesus, my Savior;
> He tore the bars away, Jesus my Lord!

> Up from the grave He arose;
> With a mighty triumph o'er His foes;
> He arose a victor from the dark domain,
> And he lives forever, with His saints to reign.[4]

The Lord Jesus is not only the source of life, He is life itself, and all other life is given and sustained by Him. He has the authority to lay down His life, and with that same authority He can take it up again. All the circumstances of His death were chosen and prophesied by Him, as was the moment

---

4. Robert Lowry, "Christ Arose," in the public domain.

when He would take His life back—opening an eye in the tomb and then another eye, taking off the wrapped grave clothes and neatly folding them, putting on a white garment to go out and meet his friends and followers, smiling with affection, talking and eating with them for almost six weeks. He had tasted death. It was inconceivable that He could be held by death even one second longer than He chose.

Jesus lay in the tomb for three days because by His death He had made an atoning sacrifice for sin. Death held Him as long as He continued to be made sin for us. But once the full price was paid, then death, Satan, and condemnation had no dominion over Him whatsoever. He had made a sacrifice of eternal and divine efficacy. It was a once and for all expiation. The sacrifice of Christ was the blood of the Son of God and so is uniquely precious in the sight of God. See the scales! On one side is the sin of the world, on the other, the blood of God, the only effective remedy for man's guilt and shame. Innumerable angels are all lost in wonder, love, and praise at what the risen Christ did once and for all.

After just three days, death lost its grip on Christ and a new phase of redeeming grace commenced in heaven. Christ began to intercede at God's right hand while the church struggled to survive, confronted by the opposition of the world, remaining sin, and the exasperated and bitter god of this world. God's plan was not only the redemption achieved by Christ but also His resurrection, exaltation, and heavenly ministry as He whispers into the ears of His Father the worthless names of all of us who have fled for refuge to Him. This was part of the plan of salvation agreed on by the Trinity before the foundation of the world, that Christ should achieve cosmic redemption and then live to apply that redemption. He must reign and complete His work of reconciliation. No other could give eternal life to favored billions save Him who had bought that life of glory for them by His agony and bloody sweat. Christ was raised; Christ ascended; Christ was enthroned at the Father's right hand with all authority in heaven and earth, and so our lives are not futile, full of sound and fury and signifying nothing; we are no longer what we once were. We possess a living hope by His resurrection and intercession, all because of His love for us that will not let us go.

How Should Man Respond to the Death of Death in the Death of Christ?

We cannot ignore death; it is looming in the future of each one of us, ever nearer with every passing moment. We are going to die, but the response of the majority of people in the world is well described in the title of cultural critic Neil Postman's book, *Amusing Ourselves to Death*. In his foreword he contrasts the dystopian visions of George Orwell (*1984*) and Aldous Huxley (*Brave New World*), and through them he paints an insightful picture of the dangers we face today:

> What Orwell feared were those who would ban books. What Huxley feared was that there would be no reason to ban a book, for there would be no one who wanted to read one. Orwell feared those who would deprive us of information. Huxley feared those who would give us so much that we would be reduced to passivity and egoism. Orwell feared that the truth would be concealed from us. Huxley feared the truth would be drowned in a sea of irrelevance. Orwell feared we would become

a captive culture. Huxley feared we would become a trivial culture.[5]

Our world is Orwellian *and* Huxleyan, but Huxley's concern is relevant here. Death is drawing steadily nearer, and the response of men is to ignore this reality and immerse themselves in what amuses them—until they are dead. We have become trivial, and triviality numbs us to the meaningful. If something is significant to you, then weigh it, considering whether it teaches you how you are to prepare for the certainty of death. What should we care about? As Paul exhorts us in Colossians, "Set your minds on things above, not on things on the earth" (3:2). What is above? God and His heaven. Who is above? The Lord Jesus Christ, the one who never trivialized death but ultimately overcame it through His own death and resurrection. Do not trivialize the Lord Jesus Christ by the clutter of amusements, claiming your right to do so as something indifferent to man and God. Is there anything that is indifferent today? Everything is posted, liked, commented on, and retweeted. We are slowly being conditioned to treat worthy things unworthily or, worse, to stop caring about anything, even the preacher of the Sermon on the Mount, the one who when crucified prayed for those who had nailed Him to the cross, saying, "Father, forgive them, for they do not know what they do" (Luke 23:34).

The Roman centurion in charge of the Golgotha horror heard these words, felt an earthquake, saw the hours of darkness, heard the last shout of Jesus, confirmed His death, and supervised His being taken down from the cross. What was

---

5. Neil Postman, *Amusing Ourselves to Death* (New York: Penguin, 1985), xix.

his response to all that? He "feared greatly." And what did this battle-weary man, exposed to such cruelty, say? "Truly this was the Son of God!" (Matt. 27:54). He had finally met reality. At the cross the ground is always level. Students and their professors, Democrats and Republicans, men and women of different races, soldiers and pacifists alike all find level ground where they can kneel before the Christ who in His dying agony prayed for the forgiveness of men. My bowing before Him and becoming His disciple is salvation and eternal life. I cannot give Him enough respect, admiration, honor, adoration, praise, and glory. To know Him is to give Him my soul, my life, my all. And as He is exalted, so, too, death is degraded, debased, and demeaned. So what do we do in response?

We Taunt Death

"O Death, where is your sting? O Hades, where is your victory?" (1 Cor. 15:55). The apostle Paul taunts death. We stand with him, not in defiance or in a refusal to admit death's solemn reality but rather with our conviction that the grave does not possess the last word. The one who claimed "I am the resurrection and the life" and "I have the keys of Hades and of Death," His is the last word (John 11:25; Rev. 1:18). On the third day He rose from the dead. Death was defeated. We who believe in Him are now raised to newness of life. Of course, if Christ tarries, then we will sleep in Jesus, to awake in blessedness. The first face we see will be His, and the first voice His. The one who said, "Lazarus, come forth!" will also raise us up (John 11:43).

It means we stop standing alongside the world in its fear of or denial of death. It means we don't need to do the crazy midlife crisis thing of getting a hair transplant, or a nose job, or buying a sports car, or beginning a relationship. It means looking more to the risen Christ and facing up to death when it intrudes into our family or circle. We stop avoiding funerals. We don't try to change the subject.

Taunting death doesn't mean we don't grieve death. I miss my parents and my first wife. I wish I had been a much better son and husband, but I do not grieve without hope. My precious ones hoped in the Lord. I believe they will be raised to life more glorious and beautiful than we ever knew here. I look forward to our reunion.

Taunting death means we honestly face the reality that we will die. It means we "number our days" (Ps. 90:12) and realize the precious gift of each one. It means speaking with our families about our death and how we want that to be a testimony to our resurrection hope. And it means we are willing to take risks of faith in this life, knowing we are utterly secure in Christ, whether it is giving generously, or getting out of our depth in witnessing to our faith, identifying with an open-air preacher, or traveling to a distant country to assist a family working there in church planting. Consider how in days of the Black Death in London Puritan preachers remained in the metropolis, visiting and praying with their dying church members. Missionaries have gone to leper colonies and some have caught the disease themselves, but they were at peace identifying with their brothers and sisters who were sick. Death does not have the victory. The triumph belongs to the one who said, "I am the resurrection and the life" (John 11:25). We taunt death.

We Delight in Hope

The word that comes from the Christian church is one of affirmation, consolation, and optimism in contrast to the sheer lack of hope and the pervasive prevalence of despair seen in the rest of humanity. How heavy the weight of gloom and despondency. Many are camouflaging that hopelessness by involving themselves in the world of commerce and by immersing themselves in amusements and relationships. Many are the prisoners of atheistic philosophies and a worldview that terminates in being snuffed out into the state of nonexistence at death. We are not called to intensify that despair. The great need of our fellow men is for light, truth, meaning, and hope. Yes, let the world know the categorical imperatives of the law of God and the solemn sanctions of death and the accompanying evaluation of our lives, but we are never to forget that the great distinctive of the Christian faith is the triumph over death of the Son of God. We do not join our voices with the chorus of the media in condemning those who have wrecked their lives by excess. We are not called to be the traffic wardens of the world but rather its light. We are offering the hope of truth, and the forgiveness of our sins, and the inheritance of God's great promises, of knowing Christ's rest and His life in us. Death is not the end but is rather the moment when the soul's courtship with God ends and there begins the unlimited face-to-face union and friendship with Jesus Christ in the world to come. To be absent from the body is to be present with Him (2 Cor. 5:8). Our full hope is of the resurrection of our bodies, when we will exchange bodies of humiliation and receive new bodies conformed to Christ Himself. What hope!

We so often forget that what leads people to repentance is not fear but the hope that there is room in the Father's house for them. An unbeliever hears that there is mercy in Christ, and so he turns from his sin and unbelief and grasps God's mercy because there is offered to him hope through the resurrection of Jesus Christ.

We Anticipate Reunion with Those in Christ
Often it is asked whether we will know one another in heaven, and frequently we respond to the effect that we are not going to be more ignorant in heaven than we are here on earth. When Jesus told the story of the rich man and Lazarus, He explained that those in the different eternal states all recognized one another—Abraham, the rich man, and the beggar Lazarus. After death they retained the unique identities of whom and what they had been before the grave.

In heaven we will have come home, and what is a home if family members do not recognize one another? Wouldn't it be a strange family circle if we knew no one there? In heaven we do not all become mass-produced identical figures, physically or psychologically. Our distinct names are recorded in heaven. Each of us will be a uniquely transformed human being. When Christ was raised, was He not transformed in some ways but still recognizable to the five hundred disciples He had gathered around Him during His three years of ministry? We will know those whom we have heard about and admired. Along with seeking out the Lamb of God who has been our Savior, our teacher, and our shepherd, we will turn and look to see again those we have loved waiting in anticipation—parents, spouses, siblings, closest friends, dear pastors, all our heroes. We will enter a new heavens and new earth together with them, rejoicing in perfect harmony.

We Will Experience Being Raised with Him in Newness of Life
Those who come to Christ have a living relationship with God. They do not live their spiritual lives vicariously or try to merely copy the outward actions of their spiritual heroes. They grow in grace, in spite of doubts. Personal sanctification happens in the lives of all the elect. There are spurts of growth, inevitably faster in the early years, but there is an ongoing relationship with the living Christ, with a growing assurance of His love and a constant awareness of His goodness.

God has heard the prayers of those who trust in Him. He has met our needs. He has overlooked our unfaithfulness. He has hidden our sins from those who loved us the most. His grace has helped us in a variety of circumstances and needs. His perfect strength has been given to match our weakness. Our deep fears were never realized. God has poured down on us blessing after blessing.

Our experience was this, that we cried to Him and He answered because He is a loving and gracious parent to us. He treated us as joined to Jesus in His life and death as such union demanded. And that confirmed for us the reality of the penal substitution, humiliation, propitiation, redemption, reconciliation, and satisfaction of Christ. There is much in the world that I can doubt today, but not that God the Son became the Lamb who stood in my stead and dealt with my condemnation. I cannot doubt the goodness of God to me. I cannot doubt that He has led me through a long life. I cannot doubt that He has heard my own prayers.

So after acknowledging all the theistic proofs and arguments that point to a great Creator and Designer, the ultimate evidence for God is seen in world history, in the history of the Lord Jesus, and in my own history. He preached and performed wonders in Galilee, He gave sight to a man blind from birth, He delivered a man under terrifying demonic powers, He described the future of the world, He gave His life a ransom for many, He rose from the dead, He changed people and made them strong, noble, and good. He also did things in my own lifetime for me, my family, and hundreds of friends and acquaintances who have enormously enriched my life. I am abundantly satisfied with the life and death of Jesus Christ. I am overwhelmed with what He has done. I could burst and dance and shout at how He has given me a loving home and intelligence. He delivered me from the cookie-cutter religion of those who surrounded me, who were merely trying to be respectable and to do their best, one Sunday after another, year after year. He gave me the Bible. He gave me a grasp of His sovereign grace. He brought the best people and the best books into my life in a stream that shows no sign of ending but rather has become a torrent of refreshing, cleansing, irrigating, exciting delight. And I do worship the one who died on the cross and redeemed me, my Lord and my Savior, Jesus Christ.

> It is a thing most wonderful,
> Almost too wonderful to be,
> That God's own Son should come from heav'n,
> And die to save a child like me.
>
> And yet I know that it is true:
> He chose a poor and humble lot,

And wept and toiled and mourned and died
For love of those who loved Him not.

I cannot tell how He could love
A child so weak and full of sin;
His love must be most wonderful
If He could die my love to win.

I sometimes think about the cross,
And shut my eyes, and try to see
The cruel nails and crown of thorns,
And Jesus crucified for me.

But even could I see Him die,
I could but see a little part
Of that great love which, like a fire,
Is always burning in His heart.

It is most wonderful to know
His love for me so free and sure;
But 'tis more wonderful to see
My love for Him so faint and poor.

And yet I want to love Thee, Lord;
O light the flame within my heart,
And I will love Thee more and more,
Until I see Thee as Thou art.[6]

---

6. William Walsham How, "It Is a Thing Most Wonderful," in the public domain.

FOUNDATION

The Lord Jesus Christ, through the shedding of His blood on the cross, inaugurated and established the new covenant. It was the final fulfillment of God's covenantal dealings with His people and the foundation of our eternal relationship with Him.

God's covenant is a divine agreement about a relationship that the Almighty Himself has designed and established with all the people whom He has given in eternity to His Son to redeem. These are the people who have, by His grace, entrusted themselves to His Son as their own personal Lord and Savior. They have, by believing in their hearts and confessing with their lips that Jesus is their Lord and Savior, thus entered this covenant. This is the means by which an eternal relationship has been established between God and His people. Being in covenant with God means being under God's grace, and that real relationship is owned and honored by God in mercy to every one of His people. That saving status cannot be changed, modified, or broken in any way by God. God will never forfeit His covenant. In fact, He writes this covenant on the hearts of all His people. Being in covenant with God results in God the Holy Spirit entering the hearts and lives of His people. It is the energy of His Spirit that enables them constantly to return to Him, again and again, every hour of every day, even if they have to pick themselves up off the floor of guilty despondency once more. They return to walking in His will, striving anew to keep His commandments. The covenant guarantees God's ever-present help, His constant mercy and unbelievable forgiveness to every one of His sinning people.

God has bound Himself to an enduring commitment to His people. He has made up His mind, and He initiates, He pledges, He accomplishes what He has designed to do. The continuance and the consummation of His covenant dealings with us are all as certainly sure as God Himself. He cannot deny what He has planned and wrought.

There was a woman who seemed very near to the kingdom of God. But in time she fell away, and the reason she gave for giving up on Christianity was that she could not believe in a God who made the choice to save favored sinners. Why did He not save everyone? But the mind of Christ looks at men and women in a different way. They love darkness, all of them. They refuse to come to Christ for light. They will not and cannot receive the things of the Spirit of God when He brings to them the beauties of the Lord Jesus and His willingness to save them and take them to heaven. "No!" they tell Him. "Here is another excuse I use for not falling before You, that You did not choose to save every single person. For me it must be all or nothing. Those are my terms." That is part of the foolishness of the natural man who rejects the covenant of grace and lays down his terms for God to be God. Yet God persists and He plucks billions of brands from the burning, not one being worthy of such a deliverance at so great a cost to God. It would be amazing should He have saved a few and treated all the rest justly and absolutely fairly. Rather, He covenants in grace to deliver an innumerably vast company, opening His arms very widely and gathering them by the gospel to be with Him forevermore. The Lord weeps over a city that refuses to come to Him for deliverance, or over a vain woman who is saying, "You have to do it my way or I am not playing ball."

Why did God covenant to save such a vast multitude? There are basically two reasons; the first is that God is love. There is not one unloving molecule in the Father, the Son, or the Holy Spirit. He is all love, and He has always loved the world He has made, and the men and women bearing His image, though that likeness has been damaged by sin. It is His love that causes Him to enter into a covenant with this unimaginably vast number of people. They are compared to the stars in the heavens, and each one now has a covenant-keeping God as Father and Savior. But this God is also just and holy, a sin-hating God, a God who is eternal light, searching and evaluating and understanding each of us.

When we remember that God keeps His covenants, it destroys any single-dimensional picture of God that we are daily encountering all around us. What I mean is that there are many who consider God as a God of rules, a God of justice and wrath. They will even imprison, assassinate, and murder people who reject this image of the divine that they hold. But another group of people think of God solely as a God of love. He loves everybody no matter what. We all go to heaven when we die.

But the Father, Son, and Holy Spirit is the God of the covenant, and He is not one-dimensional. He is loving, sure, and He is also righteous. And the God of the covenant comes to us and confronts us with His "yes" in the midst of man's "no!" God has accomplished this incredible achievement of establishing the possibility of a lasting, saving relationship with Himself without shirking His justice or betraying any aspect of His own character. His righteousness and His pity come together in His covenant. His wrath and mercy kiss.

Why did God decide to establish a covenant with a fallen and defiant group of rebels whose every inclination was only evil continually? Again, the answer is to be found in His character alone. Salvation is of the Lord. That is what He is and what He delights to do. In Hebrews 8 the author quotes from the words of God in Jeremiah 31, where God says this of His intentions toward rebel sinners: "I will put My law in their minds, and write it on their hearts; and I will be their God, and they shall be My people" (v. 33).

God is saying, "I am making a covenant so that I can come and be with you. I want you though I have no need of you. I intend to dwell with you. I have made up My mind that you are going to dwell with Me forever in a sin-free new heavens and new earth. It will all give more eternal glory to the Son whom I adore." The covenant of saving grace announces that God has made a way to live in peace and joy with human beings. This covenant is the goal of life—being with the Lord always. That is Christianity. That was the point of the Lord Jesus Christ coming, living, dying the death of the cross, rising from the dead, ascending to heaven, and reigning and interceding next to His Father. He is exercising all the authority that His cross work has merited by saving, keeping, and glorifying all those whom the Father has given to Him.

That was the point of all those centuries of altars, sacrifices, the temple, the tabernacle, the priests and Levites. It was all profoundly Christocentric. God had promised that Christ would come. God had covenanted Christ's coming, speaking through Moses and His prophets. It was all profoundly pastoral, giving to all the true Israel of God much comfort and joy in anticipation. It was all about God saying, "I want to be with you. I want to dwell with you. And whatever I want, I achieve."

Human beings, by nature, know that there is a just God whom we have sinned against and yet whom we desperately desire to be with forever. Every single religion on the planet has a system for sacrifice, a temple, or a priesthood. Of course, they are replete with error, as are all idolatries, but at the same time there's a fragment of truth present. Mankind is suppressing the fact that it knows there is a covenant God whom we have been created to know and be with, and that we've broken His laws, and He is just. The gospel church of Jesus Christ is preaching, living, and bearing testimony to this truth; we tell the world what conscience and the general revelation of God's beauty, power, and godhead alone cannot tell them. We tell others of the God of the covenant, just as this book is telling you now as it says, "See! He's made a way back to Himself, and the answer is His grace through Jesus Christ." That gospel message is the foundation of our standing before God now and eternally.

Previous Covenants and the New Covenant
The new covenant written about by Jeremiah and realized in

the life and death of the Son of God is in essence the same covenant that God has been making again and again since the time of Adam. Although the new covenant in Jesus has a greater emphasis on grace, reveals a greater understanding of the Son of God, and has manifestly richer blessings, in its operations and essence it is the same as the covenants of the Old Testament. The efficacy of Christ's incarnation and crucifixion transcend time, extending throughout eternity.

Through the achievements of our brave Savior the Old Testament believers were saved. During the last week of His life we hear all the echoes of the administrations of the earlier covenants. Consider the Last Supper's sermon as the reading of the new covenant. Consider His carrying the cross and the erection of the cross as the building of an altar. The crucifixion of Jesus is the sacrifice. The piercing of Jesus with the spear and the flow of blood is the sprinkling of blood on the altar. This also casts light on the earlier covenants as they in turn cast light on Christ.

Let's consider how God dealt by covenant with the Old Testament believers. He made a covenant first with our father Adam: "I will make both man and woman in My image and likeness" (see Gen. 1:27). He did not think, "I am the unique, glorious, holy, loving God. No one else shall be like Me!" No! He determined to make undreamed of trillions to be like Himself, partakers of the divine nature.

He made a covenant with Noah that He not only would spare him from the flood but also would never again destroy the world, and He set a sign of His grace in the heavens by distinguishing the rainbow and letting it speak to all the world of His patient restraint. Seek Him while He may be found.

He made a covenant with Abraham that his line would become a great nation, and so the people of God in all the world today are the children of Abraham.

He made a covenant with Moses promising to make Israel into a holy kingdom of priests who should spread His blessing to the surrounding nations. He told them how they should live by His law, being the world's salt and light, and what blessings that would bring upon them.

He made a covenant with David that one day one man in the line of this king would be the Messiah. "He is going to sit on your throne," He said to David. However, a greater man than Adam, Noah, Moses, or David was required. So, in each covenant the story of redemptive history advances a little further as the Lord takes the initiative to reveal and save, culminating in the final expression of the new covenant in Jesus's blood.

Those covenants were all of grace and were built one upon the other, and with each covenant God's promises and plans to redeem His many people became clearer, even in the midst of the types and shadows. They were all preparing for the coming of the Messiah, Jesus Christ. He had to come. He had to fulfill all righteousness. He had to die to make atonement for our sins. That is how God works.

To understand the continuity between the old and new covenants we are helped in seeing the illustration Paul uses in Galatians 3:24–25. Paul writes, "Therefore the law was our tutor to bring us to Christ, that we might be justified by faith. But after faith has come, we are no longer under a tutor." The tutor, or guardian (Greek *paidagogos*), was a slave whose job it was to conduct a young boy to and from school and to supervise his conduct. When the boy grew up, a guardian was no longer needed. This analogy can help us understand better the elements of continuity between the covenants.

Once the child grew to adulthood, the guardian became obsolete, but that which the guardian taught the child is not to be ignored. Paul uses this analogy of growth from childhood to adulthood as a way of viewing the people of God throughout redemptive history. The old covenant administration was intended for the people of God in their "childhood." When the people of God reached "adulthood," this childhood guardianship was no longer needed. It is now obsolete. However, that which the guardian taught the child (God's laws) remains the same.

The New Covenant Fulfilled in the Lamb of God
Jesus was made in fashion as a man, Adam being His forefather, and He is the one whom Adam was told would crush the serpent's head. Yet He Himself would not remain undamaged in the battle. Jesus was one of the offspring of Abraham, who trusted in God and became a blessing to all nations. He is the greater Moses leading all His people as pilgrims through this barren land. He kept all the laws of Moses, the moral laws, the ceremonial laws, and the civil laws as that old covenant was drawing to a close. He was the royal son of David, but He is not only the king of the Jews but King of the kingdoms of this world, and He shall reign for ever and ever. Now He sits with all authority on the throne of glory at God's right hand.

The Son of Man came in the flesh and perfectly fulfilled all that God demands. He came in a lowly position, and He was tempted in all points as we are—yet without sin. He was born into a groaning world, not into a paradise as Adam was. He was tried and tested daily as we are, in every part of His life, and yet came through them all, day by day, unblemished, never needing to say, as we do virtually each day as we put our heads on the pillow, "Sorry, Father, for the sins of commission and the sins of omission of this day." He delighted in keeping the law of God in perfection. He loved God with all His being; He loved His neighbor as Himself. He fulfilled every demand of all the covenants of God from His heart, with no reluctance or mere formalism. He could say, "Oh, how I love Your law!" (Ps. 119:97). Fulfilling a genuine human righteousness, yet doing so as the God-man, resulted in this righteousness being also divine, infinite, eternal, unchangeable, and more than enough to cover our unrighteousness. So when Satan comes and points to our sin, we respond by pointing to the righteousness that Christ has imputed to us. When Satan makes accusation of us to God, then God merely replies, "Behold the righteousness of the man Christ Jesus, My Son, who now sits at My right hand. He is their head, and where the head is, then inescapably the body also is destined one day to be." In the new covenant, God is at peace with all who are its beneficiaries through what His Suffering Servant did.

The Covenant Is Both Unconditional and Conditional

God speaks to His covenant people and tells them He has saved them: "Jesus, My Son, bled and died to redeem you. I have rescued you. You are My people. You are My treasured possession. You are My covenant people. I will not leave you. I will not forsake you." Their safety and security is 100 percent the result of His immutable salvation. But God also says,

"If you obey and you keep My covenant, then you will be My treasured possession, you will be My people forever" (see Ex. 19:5). So we have covenant language that is both unconditional and conditional.

This is what we come across throughout the Bible: the sovereignty of God and the responsibility of man. Both are always there. It is on the one hand wholly unconditional, a matter of sovereign accomplishment, but it is also a matter of going on trusting and obeying, presenting our bodies as a living sacrifice to God. There has to be both.

If the covenant were conditional on our works alone, if God came to be in relationship with us on the grounds of our obedience, then we would have a religion of legalism, ticking the boxes at the end of each day. The covenant would demand, "Obey me fully if you want to be accepted." There would be no assurance. If, on the other hand, God came and said, "I'll be your God no matter what you do, no matter how you live," then that would encourage cheap grace, easy-believism, and lawlessness. In other words, "I'll accept you no matter what you do, no matter what idols you worship, no matter what god you believe in." That would be formalistic outward religion without a walk with God.

So is the new covenant in Jesus's blood unconditional or conditional? The answer is that it is unconditional for those who have repented and entrusted their lives to the Lord Jesus because such lives are conditioned on His life and His work on the cross. It is unconditional for them because all the conditions have been met by Jesus of Nazareth. But if they are in His covenant, then the fruit of His indwelling will effectually be shown in them. They will know the filling of the Holy Spirit and the longing to keep His commandments.

Our God of the covenant comes to dwell with men by way of priesthood, sacrifice, and temple. We see that over and over again throughout the Bible. Both in the old covenant and the new covenant we have all those elements—priesthood, sacrifice, temple. In the old covenant you see the Aaronic priesthood; a sacrificial system under Moses, the blood of bulls and goats; and a temple built in Jerusalem or a tabernacle that moves with the people of Israel. But in the new covenant, too, there is a deep continuity. There is a high priest, there is a temple, and there is a sacrifice. The elements are the same. There's a deep continuity in all the covenants. In fact, there is one gracious covenant, one work that God has always been doing. It's always been the same work. It's always been about one thing.

Of course, there is discontinuity. There are things that are discarded, no longer the same in the new as once they were in the old covenant. In the Old Testament the high priest would die and the next man would take his place. Whenever he would enter into God's presence, the high priest was guilty; he needed to make sacrifices for himself to be able to work as a bridge maker between God and the people. How different is our priest. We have a high priest whose work is completely effective. He is holy and He doesn't grow doddery and infantile in old age. He lives in the power of an endless life! He's sinless, and death could not hold Him. We have a high priest just like the old covenant had, but He is indescribably better.

We have a better temple where God now chooses to live, but not one made by hands. He indwells us, and our bodies are the temple of the Holy Spirit. We now have access to the real presence of God by the blood of Christ, and we can run to a smiling Father anytime and anywhere, and He welcomes us warmly.

In this expression of the new covenant of grace we also have a sacrifice. We plead the Lamb of God who has taken away not simply the sin of the Jews but the sin of all those in the Gentile world who believe in Him. And the sacrifice He made is incomparably great, not the blood of lambs and goats but His own blood on Calvary. The true High Priest has offered His own holy self as a sweet-smelling sacrifice, acceptable to the God of light. Isn't that immeasurably better than the parade of many, many, many sacrifices for some people each hour of daylight? In the Old Testament, everyone who believed could come to the temple to bring their bulls, their goats, and their turtledoves. Hundreds of sacrifices performed by scores of priests and Levites meant that rivers of blood flowed. But in the new covenant you have a single sacrifice made by one priest, never, never to be enacted again. The cross is once for all. Christ alone died for all His people. We've moved from many priests for some people to one sacrifice and one priest interceding at the right hand of God for all the multitudes of believers who plead His name.

In the covenant of grace, the Lord Jesus is saying "Yes" to you who come in His name and plead the merit of all He has done. His grace and His promises are all "Yes" to you. The perfect, holy, indestructible High Priest has made Himself the once-for-all sacrifice satisfying all the terms of our covenant-keeping God. The covenant was conditioned upon the Lord Christ, and so now it is not "If you go on doing good and serving Him, you will be saved." No! But doing good and serving Him is the fruit of the salvation He has given to you. He went to great lengths to bind Himself to us for eternity. This He has achieved at such personal cost because He chose to love sinners like you and me.

So, are we saved by works in the new covenant? The answer is, "Yes, indeed, but they are not *our* works." We are saved by faith in the work that our High Priest accomplished perfectly and thoroughly. He did it all. We are saved by His works through our union with Him. Do you believe this? All the benefits of the saving work of Christ, especially an eternal covenant relationship with God, are ours as we put our trust in this eminently trustworthy Lord. "Why should I let you into My heaven?" asks God. The beneficiaries of the new covenant answer immediately, "Because of Jesus!" So the Lord is challenging you, "Face up to this! Please! This cross is genuine; this death happened; this sacrifice of the Lamb of God is the real thing." And then faith responds, "I rest in this. I trust in this. This is my God and Savior. This is the covenant for me." That's faith. You become a new covenant Christian by faith alone.

Do you believe it? Do you have faith in this? The new covenant probes you. And if your hopes are wholly in the work of Christ your Lord and Savior, you are now freed from guilt and condemnation. Full stop. According to the new covenant, what sadly happened in all your yesterdays is for yesterday. It cannot bind you. It is all forgiven, pardoned, and remembered by God no more. Whatever you did and whatever you did not do, yesterday is yesterday. Those sins are forgiven sins. They are gone in the promise of the new covenant.

Then be prepared for God to put His word, His precepts,

and His promises increasingly clearly into your mind as He writes them on your heart. The Lord Jesus said that He would send the Holy Spirit to dwell with His people, to speak to us, to teach us the way and enable us to do what God requires (John 14:15–18).

If the temple is God's sacred dwelling place, then our bodies have become a temple of the Holy Spirit! We are the ones who now live sacred lives. The law written on our hearts teaches us how to live, and the Spirit constantly strengthens our obedience. In other words, new covenant people are all about faith but also all about holiness. Faith in Christ and holy living are conjoined. We are not legalists. The new covenant will not let us become legalists; our eternal life was a gift of grace. We have been forgiven by the works of the High Priest, not our own. It is impossible, then, for us to become either legalists or antinomians. The blood of Christ will not let us. We live out that atonement. We want the glory of God; we want the face of God; we want to find the good for our own lives.

Live for the cross of Christ. Live your life under the protection of the blood. Live in fellowship with the Holy Spirit and then, as Martin Luther once shockingly said, "Believe in Jesus Christ and do whatever you want." What did he mean? If you're believing in Jesus Christ and you've got the Spirit changing your heart and energizing you, then your actions will flow from a renewed heart. You are constrained to do whatever the new spirit within you directs you to do, day by day. You pick yourself up after every fall and you go back on the narrow path of honoring God.

If you're following the way of Christ, then you live the way you fundamentally want to live because you're living in His way. In other words, the new covenant says to every single one of us, "God made the first move. He has gone to great lengths to bind Himself to us." And so, if we believe this, then the only legitimate response is to give ourselves to Him, to surrender, to be self-sacrificial. He will help us, especially when we fail to do the good we want to do and instead do the evil things we do not want to do. The Spirit of God is there at that moment helping our deliverance. We know an unconditional salvation, thank God, but we are being called to surrender ourselves to Him day by day in the pursuit of the holiness that pleases our covenant-keeping Lord.

Our foundation in our relationship with God is the cross of His dear Son; we rely on Him and we can look back to His mighty accomplishments for us and in us, despite all our weak faith and many falls. But covenant grace has triumphed in us hitherto, and that same grace will lead us home. We are looking forward to the time and place where we will, without any hindrance, follow the law of the Lord ceaselessly. We look forward to a time when we will be genuine and true in every respect.

We live in the time and season of the new covenant. We also live in a time that we judge to be "an overlap of the ages," where we have tasted of the heavenly thing—and, oh, what a delicious taste that is—but we long for the wedding feast of the Lamb. We live in the new covenant age in a time of faith in our crucified, risen, and exalted King Jesus who gave His life for us, and we anticipate the day when we will all meet at His feet.

12

PROCLAMATION

The cross of Christ is God's pulpit declaring the way of life.

Many things in our lives would be unseemly and unnecessary to share with the world, such as the intimacies of a husband and wife; the marital tensions and hurts; our past falls, including details of the people we hurt and how we did it; and even the amount of money we have in our bank account. Other people do not need to have such information.

We are told few if any details about many of the people Jesus meets in the Gospels. For example, the details of the killing of John the Baptist are unknown to us—who the men were who entered the dungeons and came to his cell, what they said when they took him out, where they beheaded him, how his disciples came to know about his death. Such facts are not revealed.

The death of Jesus Christ is very different. The final week of His life is described in much of the Gospels. His killing was performed in the traditional place of public executions, outside the walls of the city of Jerusalem, open to anyone who wanted to spectate. The mob was there, but also a few of His female disciples who loved Him. The mob with its taste for cruelty and violence was joined on Golgotha by the high priests, who were determined to make sure that no sudden coup might result in our Lord being stolen away at the last minute. It was indeed Jesus of Nazareth whom they hated passionately, the preacher of the Sermon on the Mount, who hung and suffered there. So those leaders watched everything closely, wanting to see Him breathe His last so that they would be satisfied in being rid of Him forever. Some of the Roman legionnaires gambled, while others watched closely and were mightily impressed with the one on the center cross. His death was announced and so His legs were not broken like those of the criminals on each side of Him. His burial place was announced by Joseph of Arimathea to Pilate the Roman governor, who seems to have been surprised that the Lord Jesus had already breathed His last. From the time His public ministry commenced, little of the life, death, and resurrection of Jesus of Nazareth was done in a corner. This is the proclamation we sing to one another and to the world.

> All ye that pass by,
> To Jesus draw nigh:
> To you is it nothing that Jesus should die?
> Your ransom and peace,
> Your surety He is:
> Come, see if there ever was sorrow like His.[1]

The author of Hebrews wrote, "It was *fitting* for Him, for whom are all things and by whom are all things, in bringing many sons to glory, to make the captain of their salvation perfect through sufferings" (2:10, emphasis added). In other

---

1. Charles Wesley, "Faith's Claim," in the public domain.

words, God's eternal decision to achieve our salvation through the sufferings of His beloved Son Jesus Christ is not arbitrary or whimsical or meaningless, but it is due to a profound fitness, appropriateness, and suitableness as the living God judges all things. Ultimately, you might say, it is beautiful. That is, it's in perfect harmony with all of God's other acts and plans. Let those words in Hebrews fly like a great banner over the sufferings of Christ. It was fitting—right, good, suitable, beautiful—in the mind of God for our salvation to be accomplished this way and not any other way.

It has often been pointed out correctly that Christianity is a religion of history and facticity, not a religious system of mysticism requiring journeys to visit gurus in caves on the other side of the world. It is not a religion demanding oaths of secrecy, as is the practice of Freemasonry and certain Hollywood religions. The religion of Jesus Christ is not one where men sit with their legs crossed, chanting vowel sounds repetitively and talking of finding nirvana. Christianity is rooted and grounded in historical fact. Golgotha was a place where a degree of latitude crossed a degree of longitude on our planet. The Christian revelation has nothing to do with myths and legends or even abstract reasonings; it is founded wholly on events in space and time and the testimony of those who witnessed it all. The writers of the Gospels, the book of Acts, and the Epistles were eyewitnesses of Jesus's majesty. The sheer factuality of the New Testament is the Alpha and the Omega of the Christian revelation.

To disprove the Bible and Christianity, one must face the facts of history and show them to be untrue and thus invalid. I fear that sometimes we forget that the Bible bases all its spiritual truths on historical events. If we allow the Bible to speak, it does not propagate nebulous abstracts but rather stubborn history. It lays the evidence bare for all to see—places, events, and people. The only reason to become a Christian is that the good news of Jesus is true. Jesus died as the Lamb of God. He rose on the third day.

So the cross of Jesus Christ, Paul says, is a declaration. It was good news, and good news must be shared, something that makes you grab the phone and tell what you know to your family and your neighbors. This news of Jesus's death is especially preachy! We do not give tips, or advice, or a description of our feelings when we stand in the name of Jesus Christ behind an open Bible. We declare the gospel of the cross, and it is utterly relevant to all the fallen sons of Adam who have ears to hear. We possess the best news of all and speak about hope for all the world to hear. The true church must fulfill its vocation in proclaiming the gospel of Jesus Christ and Him crucified. Christians can go to everyone with the knowledge that we have something simply magnificent to share with them. "I have good news for you!" is our conviction. "Behold! The Lamb of God who takes away the sin of the world!" (John 1:29).

We return again to these inspired words, "For the message of the cross is foolishness to those who are perishing, but to us who are being saved it is the power of God" (1 Cor. 1:18). We preach this message from the rooftops, on the streets, at the fairs, on the beaches, and outside casinos. Just a few verses later, Paul once again affirms, "For I determined not to know anything among you except Jesus Christ and Him crucified" (2:2). The apostle came to a resolute decision, whenever he was among them—chatting, fellowshipping, instructing, and encouraging—that he would not be long surrounded by members of the Corinthian church before he would open up the theme of the dying love of Jesus Christ. He knew how valuable it would be to remind them about it. God is sovereign in all things, and all our peace and security and hope come to us via the cross. Calvary has saving power for those who still do not believe, but it is also sanctifying to the most mature and moral of Christians, because those who know best what the Lord Christ achieved on Calvary are hungering and thirsting to hear more of it. It is a life-transforming proclamation. And it is so for that one basic reason, that it is true. We are transformed by the power of its truthfulness.

So we are summoned by the great commission of the Son of God to the foolishness of evangelism, and though it is often pointed out that it is the message itself that is folly, it also must have implications for the very action of standing up on a city street or on a beach before men and women and speaking loudly, clearly, enthusiastically, persuasively, and earnestly to those standing or passing by about the crucified Jesus Christ. "Foolishness!" mocks the world with its distorted affections. Yet proclaim we will. Christians in evangelical congregations still sing from the heart these words:

> Happy, if with my latest breath
> I may but gasp His Name,
> Preach Him to all, and cry in death,
> "Behold, behold the Lamb!"[2]

---

2. Charles Wesley, "Jesus! The Name High over All," in the public domain.

We are to be "instant" in making this proclamation of the Lord Jesus both in season and out of season (2 Tim. 4:2 KJV). To be instant means we are not standing wondering what we are now going to say to people. We have this word given carefully to us by God. It is all we need, and we are ready to speak immediately about the reason for our hope because we're enabled by God's love, power, and authority.

To everyone we meet we ultimately want to explain this message of the crucified Lord—with words. What folly the jokey phrase, "Tell people the gospel; if necessary, use words!" Words are essential in explaining the wondrous cross. Of course, we display, usually quite unconsciously, the transforming power of the Lord's death in us by how we live our lives day by day. But we do spell it out. It is on our lips, and from our hearts, even if we talk with a lisping, stammering tongue. We cannot be silent. We have no choice in the matter.

Alas, we admit there are times when we do not want to talk of our Savior's dying love. The flesh is weak. Talking of Jesus is one of the most difficult things in the world. We feel utterly inadequate to be the heralds of almighty God, but we are under divine constraint, and our debt to Him is unimaginable. We have been sent to announce the dying love of the Son of God. The message of Jesus Christ and Him crucified is the very heart of Christianity to be commended and advanced in every circumstance, and God has ever honored such a message. We become all things to all men in order to explain to everyone the cross of Christ.

CONCLUSION

Do you understand at last, at long last, what Jesus was saying when He said that no man comes to the Father but by Him, that He alone is the way, and the truth, and the life (John 14:6)? Do you understand now how He could insist on that? The only way to heavenly life is through the dying love of the Lamb of God. No one else could pay the price of sin. He alone could unlock the door of heaven and let us in. Only by Him. Mohammed, and Buddha, and the gods of the Hindus did not give their lives that we might be saved. The Lord Jesus Christ must save or we are forever lost.

What I am asking of you now is this, to bring your intellect to this word of the cross and believe it. Receive this mind-blowing truth of the historic existence and humbling of the God-man who died on Golgotha. Cling to it. Commit yourself to it. Come from where you are and place your hand, as it were, on the head of the Lamb of God. Take this posture to the throne of God and say, "Father, forgive me, because I've heard there's this blood of your Son that can make the foulest person clean. Now that blood has become my only plea. I flee from all my sins and all my virtues to hide in the wounded side of Jesus Christ, who is now my Lord and Savior. All my joy is found concentrated, spelled out, and experienced in the word of the cross. And all my sadness and shame are because of those things, that it took the cruel nails and the crown of thorns and the darkness and His abandonment to reconcile Yourself to me and obtain divine pardon for what I have been and done, but also this—that I took so long to come to Him!" The cross of the Lord Jesus Christ overwhelms. It breaks our hard hearts. It crushes and melts them, transforming them into hearts of undying gratitude and awesome anticipation of seeing the face that was spat on for us, that bore the crown of thorns for us, whose dying love took our condemnation.

> And from my stricken heart with tears
> Two wonders I confess,
> The wonders of redeeming love
> And my unworthiness.[1]

---

1. Elizabeth Cecilia Clephane, "Beneath the Cross of Jesus," in the public domain.